Studies in South Indian Architecture
(with special reference to Kerala & Tamil Nadu)

Samīkṣikā Series
No. 7

General Editor
V. Srinivas
Joint Secretary
Ministry of Culture,
Govt. of India
and Officiating Director
National Mission for Manuscripts

The Samīkṣikā Series is aimed at compiling the papers presented by the various scholars during the seminars organized by the National Mission for Manuscripts. The seminars provide an interactive forum for scholars to present to a large audience, ideas related to the knowledge contained in India's textual heritage.

In keeping with the title, the Samīkṣikā (research) Series is concerned with research papers of distinguished scholars and specialists in different intellectual disciplines of India.

Studies in South Indian Architecture

(with special reference to Kerala & Tamil Nadu)

Edited by

K.G. Sreelekha

National Mission for Manuscripts

Dev Publishers & Distributors

Published by:
National Mission for Manuscripts
Indira Gandhi National Centre for the Arts
11 Man Singh Road
New Delhi 110 001
Phone: 91 11 2307 3387
E-mail: directornamami@nic.in
Website: www.namami.nic.in

and Co-published by:
Dev Publishers & Distributors
2nd Floor, Prakash Deep,
22, Delhi Medical Association Road,
Darya Ganj,
New Delhi-110002
Phone : 011-43572647
e-mail: devbooks@hotmail.com
website: www.devbooks.co.in

ISBN 81–904029–6–X (Series)
ISBN 978-93-80829-08-1 (Vol. VII)
First published 2015

Contents

Preface

The Oriental Research Institute and Manuscripts Library is a department of the University of Kerala which was originated in the year 1903 by the Maharaja of Travancore, His Highness Sri Moolam Tirunal in order to edit and publish the manuscripts of the Royal Palace. Since then it grew in its magnitude and importance by the fosterings of the different Maharajas of Travancore who were patrons of art and literature. The department became a part of the University when the University of Travancore was established in the year 1937. Now our collection has in total above 65,000 works; 80% of which are palm-leaf manuscripts. Others include *Agarutvak, Bhurjapatra,* Copper Plates and paper manuscripts. The collection found in this department is the second largest in our entire continent. It covers every field of human wisdom like Veda to Mīmāṃsā, Nyāya, Kāvya, Rūpaka, Campu, Tantra, Mantra, Astronomy, Astrology, indigenous systems of medicine, Physics, Chemistry and even complicated forms of Trigonometry. Most of the works are in Sanskrit, others include Malayalam, Tamil, Bengali, Marathi, Gujarathi, Kannada, Telugu, Oriya etc. The scripts include ancient scripts like Nandīnāgarī, Grantha, Brāhmī, Vattezhuthu and others like Deveanagari, Marathi, Telugu, Oriya etc.

The Department now performs multifarious functions such as academic activities—the department conducts M. Phil Manuscriptology Programmes, teaches ancient scripts to Post Graduate students of other faculties as elective subjects. Also the collection of manusripus is an ongoing process in the department. We collect, catalogue and preserve them for the posterity. We also publish the manuscripts on the basis of their importance and demand from researchers. The Ph.D theses of this department are mainly critical editions of unpublished manuscript from our collection.

From the last quarter of 2003, the very year of its establishment, the National Mission for Manuscripts rejuvenated this department by giving its helping hand. Since then, this institution has gained the status of a Manuscripts Resource Centre and recently, in 2011 it has been declared as a Manuscript Conservation Centre also by the National Mission for Manuscripts. With new speed, we are moving towards our aim being consolidation and preservation of the textual heritage of out past for the posterity. We conduct surveys, catalogue and collect manuscripts, provide awareness programmes, conducted classes on paleography and preservation, help private repositories in preservation of their collection as part of the Manuscripts Resource Centre and Manuscript Conservation Centre Projects.

Since the year 2010, National Mission for Manuscripts has started helping us more in academic activities by organizing national seminars through which we are reaching out to the public more effectively by bringing into light our treasure house of knowledge. Through these seminars, we are giving emphasis to our unpublished works in a particular/specific area. The National Seminar on Manuscripts related to Architecture sponsored by the National Mission for Manuscripts is the second in the series of National Seminars. The contribution of Kerala to the field of Architecture is remarkable whether it be temple, dwelling house or huge building. Our main objective is to bring to light our collection of unpublished work related to traditional architecture and bring an awareness to those who are related to the field of architecture so that they can incorporate the advantages of ethnic style into the present constructions as demanded by modern society. The papers which were presented in the Seminar and were subjected to discussions and deliberations have been strung together with utmost care in this collection. They are mostly based on the ancient rules, principles and techniques of building making; some papers could penetrate into the most modern techniques of architecture also. Hope this work would open up new dimensions in the field of Architecture.

DR. K.G SREELEKHA
Project Co-ordinator ORIML MRC &
Prof. & Head, ORI & Mss. Library,
University of Kerala, Kariavattom

14th November, 2014

Foreword

Manuscripts in India go back a long way in history with centuries of different writing cultures and practices making their way into the textual traditions of the country. This pluralism in experience, thought and practice has led to the flowering of diverse manuscript traditions reflecting various canons of critical thinking and historiography. To promote research and interest in Indian knowledge systems with particular emphasis on manuscripts, the Mission organizes national level seminars. Scholars specializing in various fields are invited to present research papers which are eventually published by the Mission under the title Samikshika. The objective is not only to know about the existing information and practices about manuscripts but also to bring to light relatively unknown knowledge. The Mission then tries to develop and incorporate these insights into its activities.

The current Samikshika volume presents the proceedings of the seminar on "Studies of Indian Architecture in Kerala and Tamilnadu." The seminar was organized in the Oriental Research Institute & Manuscripts Library, University of Kerala under the supervision of Prof. K.G. Sreelekha, Project Coordinator and Head, DRI & MSS Library.

Different types of architectural styles showcase diversity of expressions. This volume presents the South Indian School of Architecture specially in Kerala and Tamil Nadu and covers Temple as well as Building Architecture. The architectural content in the Works of other disciplines like

Arthaśāstra and Nāṭyaśāstra have also been discussed in the respective papers.

This volume should prove quite useful to the readers in general. I wish to thank to the scholars who have presented the papers and also to the publisher, Dev Publishers & Distributors for bringing out this volume.

DR. SANGHAMITRA BASU
Co-ordinator Research & Publication
National Mission for Manuscript

New Delhi
24th December, 2014

Key to Transliteration

VOWELS

अ a	आ ā	इ i	ई ī	उ u	ऊ ū
(but)	(palm)	(it)	(beet)	(put)	(pool)
ऋ ṛ	ए e	ऐ ai	ओ o	औ au	
(rhythm)	(play)	(air)	(toe)	(loud)	

CONSONANTS

Guttural	क ka	ख* kha	ग ga	घ gha	ङ ṅa
	(skate)	(blockhead)	(gate)	(ghost)	(sing)
Palatal	च ca	छ cha	ज ja	झ jha	ञ ña
	(chunk)	(catchhim)	(john)	(hedgehog)	(bunch)
Cerebral	ट ṭa	ठ* ṭha	ड/ड़ ḍa	ढ*/ढ़ ḍha	ण* ṇa
	(start)	(anthill)	(dart)	(godhead)	(under)
Dental	त ta	थ tha	द da	ध dha	न na
	(path)	(thunder)	(that)	(breathe)	(numb)
Labial	प pa	फ* pha	ब ba	भ bha	म ma
	(spin)	(philosophy)	(bin)	(abhor)	(much)
Semi-vowels	य ya	र ra	ल la	व va	
	(young)	(drama)	(luck)	(vile)	
Sibilants	श śa	ष ṣa	स sa	ह ha	
	(shove)	(bushel)	(so)	(hum)	
Others	क्ष kṣa	त्र tra	ज्ञ jña	ळ* l	ॠ* ṝ
	(*kṣātriya*)	(*triśūla*)	(*jñānī*)	(play)	

अं *(—) ṁ* or *ṃ amusūra* (nasalisation of preceding vowel) like *saṃskṛti/or soṃskṛti*

अः *visarga* = *ḥ* (aspiration of preceding vowel like (*prātaḥ*)

ऽ *Avagraha* consonant #' consonant (like-*imé vasthitā*)

Anusvāra at the end of a line is presented by m (म्) and not *ṁ*

*No exact English equivalents for these letters.

1

TANTRIC AND SCIENTIFIC TECHNIQUES OF TEMPLE ARCHITECTURE IN KERALA WITH SPECIAL REFERENCE TO THE TANTRASAMUCCAYA

P. Vasumathy Devi

The Indian temple of which the temples of Kerala, form the microcosm, is by unanimous verdict, the product of Indian religion and philosophy. "The mystics of India, reconciled the aims of the artist and philosopher," as E.B. Havell puts it, and with great power of technical expression, took the monumental art to "the loftiest heights ever yet attained by human thought."[1] For this attainment, the Indians adopted a scientific and mystical framework or scheme as delineated in the Agamic and Nigamic or Tantric texts as well as treatises on Architecture—the Śilpaśāstra manuals.

The textual matrix of formal architecture in India emanates from the significant Upaveda of *Sthāpatya* which in its turn through the science of *Vāstu* shower the scientific techniques of creating the choicest residences for man and abodes for gods as protectors of the land and people. The sources of architectural details of Vāstuśāstra are myriad like the Sūtra literature of the Gṛhya and the Sulba group, Purāṇas like *Matsya, Skanda, Agni* and *Viṣṇudharmottara* (forming an appendix to *Viṣṇupurāṇa),* etc. Āgamas, which are followed especially in the south of India, deal with *vāstu* rules to a considerable extent.[2] The Kāmika is largely devoted to Śilpa and Sthāpatya arts. Along with such texts, there are the Tantra literature like the *Hayaśīrṣa Pañcarātra,* Saṃhitās like the *Bṛhat-saṃhitā, Pratiṣṭhā* (installation) manuals like the *ĪśānaŚiva-gurudevapaddhati* and regular northern and southern Śilpa texts of mythical Viśvakarman and Maya authorship. Further the *Aparājitapṛcchā,* the *Rūpamaṇḍana, Samarāṅgaṇa Sūtradhāra* and *Viśvakarmaprakāśa* deal with northern style while the *Mayamata, Kāśyapaśilpa,* the *Mānasāra,* the *Śilparatna, Tantrasamuccaya,* etc. are typical texts dealing with the southern style. The Śilpa texts have scientific elements of exposition of the physical, geographical, astronomical, philosophical, mathematical and iconographical aspects of temple architecture and divine installations and everything is reduced to formulae in black and white, in a way that should prove easy to the pious entrepreneurs and practitioners. Indeed, the methodology of temple construction, its rites and ceremonies and its sociological and religious rewards, are all so explicitly documented, that a degree of unquestioning submission to the rules set out in the texts became customary.[3] Most of the Agamic texts laid out comprehensive and scientific formulae for the proportionate measurements of the constituent limbs and lineaments of the temple models, and tended to cover all the variants and atypical types.

Śilpa and Tantric texts in Kerala

Unlike in many parts of India, Kerala temples preferred the original Vaidika and non-agamic rituals with a stress on sanctity, simplicity, lack of esoteric overtones and a prevailing naturalism. Though the Kerala architects took inspiration and constructional guidance from the common fountain of the Indian Vāstu and Śilpa texts, it is interesting to find that certain manuals have a decidedly local stand and are considered to having been compiled for regional guidance. For example, the *Tantrasamuccaya* which is unanimously accepted to be greater than the earlier *Śilparatna,* is primarily intended for Kerala and spells out the regional architectural aspects in its most outstanding features.

The evolution of Tantra Siddhānta and the Tantrasamuccaya

The Vedas which are the corner stones of Indian Sanātana dharma have two main branches of realization—the *Jñānakāṇḍa* and the *Karmakāṇḍa*. The first includes the Upaniṣads and similar philosophical treatises. The Karmakāṇḍa consists of Mīmāṃsā Siddhānta of which a continuation and outgrowth in later times was the Tantric Siddhānta. Perhaps antedating the Vedic practices, the Tantra has had been in vogue in the folk religions in the various regions of the country and developed in the Tantric systems of the Mahāyāna Buddhists and the Śāktas. Traditionally of the five well-known schools of Tantra, which transcended the boundaries of present day India, the Kerala, Kashmiri and Gauda traditions were recognized as distinct.[4]

During the ages the sacred performers in Kerala developed a vastly complicated technology of worship, marked by continuity and change from the earliest 'primitive' forms to sophisticated 'modern' variants.[5] With the Brahmanical settlements in Kerala, the transformation of the pre-existing local Tantric practices and the traditions of the Buddhists as well as the left-hand practices (*Vāmācāra)* of the Śāktas were altered to a certain extent to de-emphasize the bloody and orgiastic practices and the Kerala *Sampradāya* (Kerala model) as more *sāttvika* (refined) in nature and became a kind of vedic worship in Tantric mode, though the original practices continued in certain cases. Sanskrit works like the *Śāradātilaka,* the *Prapañcasāra tantra,* the *Prayogamañjarī,* the *Īśānaśivagurudevapaddhati,* the *Rahasya-gopālatantra,* etc. became the standard works and strictly the monopoly of Brahmin practitioners. All these earlier works were incorporated into the famous and authoritative work, viz. the *Tantrasamuccaya* by Chennas Narayanan Nambudiri-pad around 1427 AD.

The Tantrasamuccaya

The *Tantrasamuccaya* of Chennas Manakal Narayanan

Namboodiripad is a compendium of the enlightened version of the Tantric system and deals with every detail of temple worship from the planning and architecture of the temple, fixing the location and site, qualifications for an *Ācārya* who shall conduct the rituals, purification and installation of structures and icons, purification and instilling of 'life' into the idol, modes of meditation, rituals, and practice for the body of the worshipper, the premises and the idol itself, the *pūjā* rites, including the daily, monthly, annual and festive rituals, and the reinstallation, reconstruction and repairs of existing temples. Two commentaries on this great work carried it forward and linked it with the earlier texts on the subject, the *Vimarśinī* (a critical review) by Chennas Sankaran Namboodiripad and the *Vivaraṇa* (description) by Krishna Sarma, one of the disciples of Chennas Namboodiripad; Krishna Sarma's another compendium—*Śeṣasamuccaya* expanded the coverage to include rites related to deities who had not been covered in the *Tantrasamuccaya*. A Malayalam commentary titled *Kuzhikkattu Paccha* composed by one Kuzhikkat Maheswaran Bhattatiri, a commentary known as *Tantrasaṃgraha* by Kelallur Chomatiri, *Kriyadeepika* by Vasudevan Namboodiri, and text called Pudayoor Bhasha, etc. have further popularized the scholarly content in the *Tantrasamuccaya*.[6] The prescriptions in these works are adopted in most temples, but with significant exception. In the ancient Tiruvalla temple, the *Śrauta Pūjā*, closely following the Vedic formulae is retained. In some Viṣṇu temples of Kerala like Śripadmanābha Swamy temple a *Paddhati Sampradāyam,* different from the *Tantrasamuccaya* is known to be followed and the main practitioners of this system of Tantra in temples belong to the Taranallur Tantris of Irinjalakkuda. The variations are said to be however not fundamental and the *Tantrasamuccaya* continues to be the undisputed authority on the subject. Though the work was composed in the fifteenth century, its contents are based on very old traditions carried forward orally from generation to generation. It was compiled on the basis of ancient texts such as the *Mayamata* of Maya and *Kāśyapīya* of Kāśyapa Maharṣī. A free translation of the *Śilpa* part of the text into Malayalam by Kanipayyur Damodaran Namboodiripad and the interpretation of the *Tantrasamuccaya* typed script of K.Rāmapisharati[7] are utilised for references in the present paper. Another free translation, *Thatchusastram Bhasha,* and edited by one Cheruvally Narayanan Namboordiri has also been of referential use to corroborate the conclusions of the *Samuccaya.*[8]

The *Tantrasamuccaya* is a comprehensive compendium and is a manual offering constant guide to the practitioners of temple rites, rituals and architectural application. It has three parts and twelve *paṭalas* or sections ranging from *Bhūparigraha* or selection of site for a temple, *Adhiṣṭhānavidhi, Ekatalavidhi, Dvitaladividhi, Bimbalakṣaṇa, Dhyānaślokas, Dhvajalakṣaṇa, Nāṭyamaṇḍapa, Gopuravidhi,* etc. Geometrical and scientific techniques are utilized for finding the directions. By a simple construction of lines the north to south axis is drawn as the *Nāḍisūtra.* From this, the directions are clearly drawn in quarters. Accurate mathematical calculations are given for measurements for the *Adhiṣṭhāna* (basement), the *Stambha* (pillar), the *Upapiṭha,* the *Padma,* measuring methods of the heights of the *Prasāda or Kṣetra,* marking of the divisions like *Garbhagṛha, Antarāla Madhyanati,* etc., the measurements for the *Garbhagṛha,* the thickness of the walls of the *Gabhagṛha* termed as *Ghanabhitti* the scheme of the outer walls, the main door or *dvāra,* the places of the *Ghanadvāras* (make-belief doors) and *toraṇas* over them, etc. It speaks of the *Vedikā* at the base as ornamented by the *Pañjaras* and the *makara* balustrade for the approach steps into the main temple. It specifies only such elements like *Oma* (basal block), *Ghaṭa, Maṇḍi, Virakāṇḍa* and *Potikās* for the pillar, thus revealing the late date of the text by which time pillar had become stereotyped. It referes to the ornate exterior of the circular sectioned *praṇāla.* In its description of the *Praṇāla, the Samuccaya* is even more explicitly suggestive of the developed mediaeval

Kerala situation. The dimensions of the door post, characteristics of the *Sopāna,* the dimensions of the *Śālās, Kūṭas,* etc. and the measurements of the *Uttira* (beam) like *Khaṇḍottara* and the rafters (*Kazhukols*), all are very precisely enumerated. The process of metal covering for the *stūpi* and the *Śikhara,* the ornamentation of the *Grīvā* and the measurements of the various parts of the *prastara*—all are scientifically depicted. Precise calculations for the dimensions of the *Ekatala, Dvitala,* and *Tritala Vidhis* of the *prāsāda* are given in measurement techniques using typical Kerala terminology. The construction techniques of square, round apsidal, elliptical, hexagonal and octagonal structures of *prāsādas* are given and the geometrical and mathematical measurements are very keenly calculated. The location of the *Mukhamaṇḍapa* and the classification of the *sanctum* according to their shape along with details of the *Pancha-prākāra* are depicted.

Pañcaprākāra

The *Pañcaprākāra* scheme of Kerala temples involves the *antarmaṇḍala* (ahatte *balibattan* or the *sanctum* chamber), *the antahara* (*cuttambalam* or *nalambalam*), *Madhya hara* (*vilaku madam* or the ambulatory on the edge of the plinth) *bāhyahara* (*Sivelippura*) and *maryādā* (*Purāmadil*). The *avatāra maṇḍala* consists of the first *Prākāra* which would be half way from the sanctum and should have 2/2 square of the *Śrīkovil.* The *Samuccaya* makes it clear how only the first and the last *Prākāra* will have a facade (*Mukhayama).* The *namaskāramaṇḍapa* should come in the middle of the *Śrīkovil* and the *Agrasabhai.* The eight *balikals* represent the *Aṣṭadikpālakas* who should face the opposite directions.[9] In most of the later temples of Kerala, the *mukhamaṇḍapa,* entirely of wood work or simplified patterns, encloses the *balipīṭha* while in many of the earlier temples, the *balipīṭha* is well outside along the eastern axis and open to the sky. In the *Madhyahara* is found the *Dīpadhāman* (cloister where the lights were lit).

Usually in South Indian temple structures, there would be an outerwall or *maryādā* with a tiered gateway (*gopūra*) for each of the *prākāra*. But in Kerala only in the last outerwall there would be a *gopūra* and the Kerala *gopūra* seldom overtop the *Vimāna*. The tiers in the gateway seldom exceed three. The notable exceptions as at Thiruvananthapuram Padmanabha Swamy temple are obviously copied from the Pāṇḍya style.

The *Tantrasamuccaya* alone is enough to prove the precise scientific technique and engineering skill followed in Kerala temple architecture. For mathematical calculations the science of *Jyotiṣa* (*Jyotirgaṇita*) became a correlative to Vāstuśāstra.[9]

Site selection and fixing of directions

One of the former sections of the *Samuccaya* deals with *bhūparigraha* or the selection of suitable site for the temple based upon specific *lakṣaṇas* and the taking charge by the *Tantri* of the spot for further ritual cleansing rites. After that, ingenious methods are used for fixing of the cardinal directions without the use of a compass. The shadow cast by the sun on successive days is measured, after applying corrections according to whether it is in the summer or winter solstice. A cylindrical stake in length a *muzhakol* (a somewhat locally varied measure of length divided into *aṅgula* and may vary from 27-30 inches) is used for the measurement. After the identification of the directions, the site is formally handed over to the *Tantrī* for initiating the construction. He, after a number of rituals, starts with a ritual ploughing and sowing of seeds in the site.

The geometry and philosophy of architecture

Central to the philosophy of Indian architecture is the concept of *Vāstupuruṣa*, an anthropomorphic deified figure, imagined to be lying within the building space, with his head to the north east and his feet, pressed together, in the opposite direction. The *Vāstupuruṣa's* posture should not be disturbed and the little squares into which the site is split up in the successive quartering, are believed to be home of certain Vedic deities related to the varied aspects of a balanced cosmic energy. Depending on the posture of the site, geometric variations are permissible but care is to be taken that the relative orientation of these auspicious deities is unaltered. The *Vāstupuruṣa's* benevolent existence for the generation of positive cosmic energy is achieved by a balance of construction and open spaces within the site which "functionally promotes adequate ventilation and aesthetic harmony."[10]

Like all the significant Indian treatises on Architecture, the *Tantrasamuccaya* also keeps up the scheme of the science of *vāstu* in laying the geometric and conventional rules of temple architecture. The geometric principles underlying the concept of *vāstu* have cosmic significance, the east west diagonal representing the ecliptic along which the sun and the moon apparently traverse, it is thus the *bhrāmavīthi* or the cosmic path. The twelve squares adjacent to it represent the twelve signs of the zodiac each with its presiding deity. The area outside these can be further demarcated into the eight positions of the cosmic quatrains—the *aṣṭadikpālakas.* Thus the temple site is a microcosm recreating the Universe in the middle of which the icon representing the deity is to be installed and the space is reserved for *Brahmā,* the creator of the Universe.

Measurements and Scientific precision of structures

In the *paṭalas* or parts of the *Samuccaya* dealing with *Prākāravidhī, Adhisṭhānavidhi, Sthambhavidhi,* and the *Bimbavidhi* the scientific construction techniques are discussed and the units of measurements are mostly typical of Kerala. The usual units are *kol, aṅgula, yava, paramāṇu, trasareṇu, kiṣku, daṇḍu, nāḍikā, yoni, āya, vyāya, gaja, vyāsa,* etc. The smallest unit is *yava* (grain), next comes *aṅgula* and the greater is the *Kol.* Usually for temples just like for houses, the *kol* becomes the basic unit. A corelation units is established as following:

1 kol	= *24 aṅgula*
1 aṅgula	= *8 yava*
24 aṅgula	= *1 kiṣku*
4 kols	= *1 daṇḍu*
8 daṇḍu	= *1 ranju*
1000 daṇḍu (2.88 k/metre)	= *1 nāḍikā (nazhika)*
24 minutes	= *1000 daṇḍu* etc.

When it comes to detailing the measurements for the pillar, the *Adhiṣṭhāna,* the *Garbhagṛha,* doorway, etc., the height, breadth, and the perimeter are given in units of *yoni, aya, vyāya, nakṣatra, daṇḍa* etc. The exact scientific and mathematical precision of the temple parts was ensured through these measurements of construction. For instance when the desired perimeter was multiplied by three divided by eight the remainder thereof is *yoni,* and when divided by fourteen the remainder is *vyāyu;* again when the same is multiplied by eight and divided by twelve, the remainder is *āya;* when divided by twenty-seven, the remainder is *nakṣtra*; when divided by seven, the remainder is the day of the week and when divided by thirty the remainder is *tithi.*

An increase of *āya* over *vyāya* must always be secured; otherwise it is inauspicious. The auspociousness of *nakṣtra* etc. must be known through the science of astrology.

Parts of Adhiṣṭhāna and their proportion

After telling the methods to calculate the height of the building from the *pādukā* of the basement to the *stūpi,* the various parts of the *adhiṣṭhāna* or basement part of the temple structure and their proportions are given. The *adhiṣṭhāna* mouldings for the Kerala temples usually consist of components like the *upapīṭha, the padma (padmapādukā), jagati, Kumuda, galam, padi, vedi,* etc. The plinth combinations may vary slightly as per the varied temples and various types of measurements are provided in the *Samuccaya* for the distinct parts of the *adhiṣṭhāna.* In all descriptions there is a stipulated mathematical correlation of the dimensions of the structure of the *prāsāda* and those of the different components like the *upapīṭha, padma, kumuda, jagati* etc.

In part II of the *Samuccaya,* the *Stambhavidhi* or the rules for the disposition and construction of the pillars are given. The shape of the pillars, their components, their faces and nature of their ornamentation etc. are specified. Then the location of the door, the height and breadth of the doorway in accordance with the *garbhagṛha,* the characteristics of the *sopāna,* description of the *ghanadvāra,* the *Toraṇa* etc. form the rest of the *Samuccaya* part on *Stambhavidhi.*

Part III of the *Samuccaya* contains *Bhittividhi* or rules regarding the construction of the wall and the description of the *vedikā.* The height of the *vedikā* may be equal to that of the *prati* or one-eighth, one seventh or one-sixth of the height of the pillar. Every *prāsāda* will have pillars, *toraṇas* and four doors. For bigger *prāsāda* there will have decorations like *śālās, kuṭas, nāsikās, jālaka* and shining *pañjaras.* The *pañjaras* are to be made of the dimensions of two, three or four *daṇḍas* with *nāsikā. Jālakas* are to be constructed above the *vedi,* two, three or four *daṇḍas* in *vistāra.* The dimensions of the *kuṭas, śālās,* description of the *kumbhalata,* the peculiar ornamentation of *alpageha* etc. form the rest of the *Bhittividhi.*

Within part IV of the *Samuccaya* the characteristics of *Ekatalaprasitravidhi* are given. The measurements of the main beams (*uttara)* used in the building of *Ekatalaprāsāda* (single storied temple) are mentioned, the *khaṇḍottara* having a thickness and breadth equal to that of the *vistāra* of the pillar.

The proportions of other beams like *Rūpottara, Vajana, mahāvajana* are given. Above the beam is to be placed a *paṭṭikā* (rafter) having a breadth of the depth of the *uttara* and a thickness of half its breadth. Construction of the ceiling with wood or stones the methods of the use of rafters etc. are specified. Above the *uttarapaṭṭikā* are to be placed the rafters with their extremity secured in the *kūṭa*. The rafters are to be covered up all around with planks of good tree. Above it a *stūpi,* is to be fixed having half the height of the basement, composed of the full-blown lotus, *kumbha* etc., with its top of the shape of the fresh lotus bud. The *Śikhara* of the *Vimāna* must then be covered up with sheets of metal such as copper.

In the next part (Pt. VI) of the *Samuccaya,* the *Prākāravidhi* of *Dvitalaprāsāda* with its different measurements and construction methods are described. In part VII of *Prākāravidhi* the rest of the *Pañcaprākāra* with the techniques, scientific and philosophical principles behind each construction and the measurements in *daṇḍa* and *aṅgula* are given. Thus the *Mukhamaṇḍapa,* the dimensions of the *Balipīṭhas,* the *pūjāmaṇḍapa,* the *antahara,* the *padasudra* types of *sabhā,* etc. are delineated.

Śrīkovil (Garbhagṛha)

The *Śrikovil* (*Garbhagṛha*—the womb house) is the *sanctum sanctorum,* the epicentre of a temple. So utmost care is taken for its construction "with respect to architecture, beauty, serenity and above all security."[11] Of the five broad categories of *garbhagṛha,* square, rectaṅgular and circular types are more common in Kerala. Circular types are peculiar to southern Kerala. Rectaṅgular *Śrīkovil* are mostly those of gods like Śāstā. Apsidal *Śrīkovils* are seen in northern and central Kerala.[12] The *Tantrasamuccaya* has provided nine measurement techniques for constructing the *garbhagṛha* with its dimensions in relation to the diameter of the *prāsāda* as a whole.[13] For example, in one method it is stated that when the breadth of the *prāsāda* is divided by numbers beginning with three and ending with fifteen, the *Garbhagṛha* may be given a breadth which may begin with two parts and end with eight.[14] Each of these types of *Garbhagṛha* can be either with a solid wall or with two or three annular walls around the central chamber, i.e. the *nirantara* and the *sāntara* respectively. A variant of the *sāntara* type is represented by examples wherein the ambulatory passage is provided between *garbha* and *ardhamaṇḍapa*, going all around the former, as at Tirumittakkode temple. The *Garbhagṛha* of this famous Kerala temple is also an instance of great scientific skill being displayed by the Kerala *Śilpin* for instance, on days when the sun rises over the equinox, its rays entering through the eastern doorway into the *nalambalam,* falls directly on the idol in the *garbhagṛha.* The latitudinal degree of the sun rays, the measurements of the curves of the river infront, the degrees of the heights and depression of the region—all these aspects have been kept in mind by the genius of the architects of the temple *prāsāda* of Tirumittakode to obtain such a precision.[15]

One of the essential parts of the *Garbhagṛha* is the waterchute and the *gomukha* to carry the used water to be taken out. The water drain is to be constructed at the end of the *prati* or *gala* along the *madhyasūtra*[16] and must arise from the open mouth of a *Vyāli* adorned with necklace, wreaths, creepers etc. while its extremity must resemble the *Gomukha.* Another segment leading to the *garbhagṛha* is stated to be the *sopāna.* Beginning with the foot rest of the door and going down to the level of the land an even number of steps of *Samani* dimensions of hard stone in one and a half or two *daṇḍas* in extent, and whose either extremity is bounded by creeperine structures issuing from out of the mouth of a *Makara* situated on either side of the front door, the *sopāna* structure is delienated. The temples are so designed that beyond the *Valiabalikallu* and the *sopana* one gets a straight view of the main installed deity. All the succeeding openings are arranged in order to enable this and provide an artificial perspective lending a feeling of great depth and distance.

Idol installation and the Tantric concepts and rites

Pratisṭhānavidhī or description of the scientific and mathematical location of the exact point of installation of the idols of the temple forms a significant section of the *Samuccaya.*[17] After a cosmic and mathematical segmentation of the *garbhagṛha* into forty-nine divisions, the centremost area is called the *Brahmapāda,* surrounded by the *Devapāda, Mānuṣapāda* and the *Piśācapāda.* A further subdivision into segments is then done and the *pratiṣṭhā* (installation) will be done from the eighth segment towards the rear. The idol is to be installed with a slight deviation towards the north of the central east-west line with a further deviation towards the north-east corner. The deviations depend upon the deity to be installed and the exact directions and locations within the *Brahmapāda, Devapāda* and *Piśācapāda* where the different types of idols are to be installed with all types of *Tantravidhis* or modes of Tantric rites and rituals as detailed in the *Samuccaya.*

Tantric concepts—the Ṣaḍādhāra concepts of human body and their application in temple consecration and idol installation

From a description of the *Garbhagṛha (Śrīkovil)* and the *Pañcaprākāravidhī,* their dimensions and relative measurements and shapes based on scientific calculations, the *Samuccaya* through the succeeding *Paṭalas* (sections) deliberate on the Tantric modes of rites and rituals to recreate and modulate the cosmic energy into the concepts of *Iṣṭadevatā* (select godly form) idol of the specific temple constructed in order to be of positive benediction to the devotees concerned. Upaniṣads like the *Taittirīya* refers to the *pañcakośa* (five segments) of the *Sūkṣmaśarīra* or inner body of man. Human existential body is explained in Indian philosophy of Yoga within the two sections *Sthūlaśarīra,* (external and visible body) and *Sūkṣmaśarīra* or inner body). *Sūkṣmaśarīra* consists of *pañcakośas* (five segments)—*Annamaya, Prāṇamaya, Manomaya, Vijñānamaya,* and *Anandamaya koṣas.* Human body is totally referred to as a *Kṣetra* (temple). Just as the *pañcakośas* exist within human body (*Sūkṣmaśarīra*) so also the *Mūrtikṣetra* (*Devakṣetra* or temple) is consistent with the *pañcaprākāra.* Just as human soul, exists within the *pañcakośas* so the particular *deva* (godly concept) exists within the *pañcaprākāra* of the temple. The *pañcaprākāras* like (1) *Antarmaṇḍapa,* (akathebalivattom) (2) *Antahara,* (nalambalam) (3) *Madhyahara* (Vilakkumadam and Dīpstambha) and (4) *Bāhyahara* (*pradikṣaṇāpath* and *Seevelipura*) (5) *Maryādāprākāra* are equivalent to *annamaya-kośa, prāṇamayakośa manomayakoṣa,* etc. As the structural patterns of temples extended the surrounding walls and *gopūra* came to be constructed for all *prākāras.*

Similarly as per the *Sthūlaśarīra* (material or outer body) concept of the individual *(puruṣa)* the *Kṣetramaṇḍala* (temple region) is considered to be the bodily parts of the *kṣetrapuruṣa.* The parts of the temple from *Garbhagṛha* to the *Mukhamaṇḍapa* (*ardhamaṇḍapa*) along with the entrance wall of the temple with *gopūra* are conceived to be similar to limbs of human body. So *Śrikovil (garbhagṛha)* conceived to be the head, *antarāla* to be the face, *namaskāramaṇḍapa* to be the neck, *mahāmaṇḍapa* to be the chest and belly, *ardhamaṇḍapa* (*mukhamaṇḍapa*) to be the hands, *Valiabalikkal* (big *bali* stone) to be the thighs, and the entrance gopura to be the feet of the *deva.* As God, was regarded to be the ruler of Universal *dharma.* He was conceived to be wearing a crown equated to the dome of the temple.

The *Tantrasidhānta* conceives the *Brahmāṇḍa* (universe) or *Samaṣṭiśarīra* to be the macrocosm while the individual human body (*Vyaṣṭiśarīra*) is its microcosm. The universal soul (*mahācaitanya)* which expands through the *Samaṣṭiśarīra* referred to as Brahman or Tripurasundarī in Tantric concept and as *Yogapuruṣa* in Vaishnava concept, exists as the yogic force of *Kuṇḍalinī* in the individual body. The individual body (*Sūkṣmaśarīra*) as per Tantric yoga concept is made up of six energy circles and above all the final energy circle (*Ṣaṭcakras*) of *Sahasrāra cakra.* These are not manifest *(Pratyakṣa)* but exists in the *sūkṣma śarīra* and to be manifested only through Yogic practices of the utmost degree. The microcosmic energy of *Kuṇḍalinī* is conceived to be in a dormant state in the basic *cakra,* the *Mūlādhāra* (pelvic plexus), within the backbone (*merudaṇḍa* in Yogic concept), the three basic nerves of—*iḍā, piñgalā* and *sūṣumṇā* are conceived—*iḍā* in the left, *piṅgalā* in the right and *suṣumṇā* in the middle which is the hollow passage for the upward journey of the *Kuṇḍalinī* force woken by the dumb-found practice of *yoga prāṇāyāma dhyāna, mantra* and utmost concentration under a real *ācārya* (guru). The awakened encircled and coiled force of *Kuṇḍalinī* passes upwards awakening the six energy circles of the *Sūkṣmaśarīra*–(1) *Mūlādhāra,* (2) *Svādhiṣṭāna,* (3) *Maṇipūraka,* (4) *Anāhata,* (5) *Viśuddha,* and (6) *Ājñācakras.*

When the awakened *Kuṇḍalīnī* energy reaches the topmost circle or *Sahasrāra cakra* on top of the head, it is said the blending of Śiva-śakti or the basic forces of the universal concept occurs. According to the Tantric concept this blending of extraneous energy fills the yogī with an unexplainable state of salvation and the individual attains eternity (*jīvanmukti*).

As temple is considered to be the *Samaṣṭi* form of *Devaśarīra* (body of Deva) so before the construction and consecration of the temple, at the bottom of the selected spot for idol installation the symbols of *Ṣaḍādhāra* (six circles) are installed in stone or metal one after another. Then the *Ācārya* or main *tantrī* transforms his Yogic energy into the symbols and above it the idol is installed with necessary *pūjas,* mantras and rites to awaken the existent energy within the idol. As symbolic of the *mūlādhāra cakra* a square rock is placed deep under the exact point of the idol installation. Above the basement rock there would be made crescent shaped pit and filled with corns symbolizing the *svādhiṣṭhāna cakra* and known as *Dhyānapīṭha.* Upon it is placed a jar full of gold coins and precious stones, etc. symbolizing *Maṇipūraka cakra.* Above it an eight petalled lotus made of gold, silver and copper is placed and symbolizes the Yoga *cakra* in place of the heart or *Anāhata cakra* in supplication of God. Upon the lotus there is installed a tortoise (*Kūrma*) made of gold, silver, copper, etc., symbolizing *pañcaprāṇa* concept indicating the suppression of the five senses and concentration for Yogic uplift. The *Kūrma,* faces the facade of the *garbhagṛha.* The representation of the yogapath of the neck region (yoga nāla) in the form of a cylinder from the *Kūrma* to the surface of the earth. Upon it is placed a genderless stone—*napuṃsakaśilā* as symbolic of the formless, genderless '*sat*' or Parabrahman. It is placed after *pūjā* with innumerable chanting of necessary mantras. Upon it is placed a *pīṭha* or low dias which would be made of male stone if the idol is a female deity or a female stone if the deity would be a male one. It symbolizes the Śiva-Śakti symbiosis which is conceived according to Tantric śāstra to take place in the *Sahasrāracakra.* Indeed the *Saḍādhāra* installation is the identification of the *Sādhaka's* (devotee's) *Sūkṣmaśarīra* to be in unison with the *Devaśarīra.* It is hoped that just as the nectar of Yogic energy disseminates from a Yogī who has attained the culmination of *kuṇḍalinī saṃyoga* at *Sahasrāra,* so, Godly energy will spread over the devotees who adore the *deva* with a pure heart, a pure body and Yogic devotion.[18]

Rituals related to idol installation

Before the final adoration and *pūjā* can take place, a series of rites and rituals are to be performed as prescribed in the *Tantrasamuccaya* where the *tantrī* plays a prime role. For example the *Vāstubali* wherein the *Vāstupuruṣa* is invoked *(āvāhana)* and offerings are made once again. Before the actual installation is done, there takes place the ritual processes of *bimba parigraha, bimba śodhana, netronmilana, kautuka bandhana, maṇḍapa saṃskaraṇa, agnijanana, prāṇapratiṣṭhā, aṣṭabandha* preparation, *godohana, vaiśya homa, Prāsāda-pratiṣṭhā, kalasa-homa, parāvahana, avasthāvahana, taṭvahoma* and *kalasas,* the *pratiṣṭhā, Natakkal pūjā, Śrī Bhūtabali,* etc. in order to propitiate the chief deity as well as his or her supportive and sub deities.[19]

Conclusion

Thus a study of the significant Śilpa text of the *Tantra-samuccaya* reveals not only the scientific and Tantric aspects of temple construction but also the fundamental ideas which underlie the structure and symbolism of temple architecture and idol installation especially in relation to Kerala. It is a profound theme and further study of individual instances, techniques and variations of Kerala temples and idols, is needed for a deeper understanding of the scientific and tantric technologies underlying the sacred traditions and rhythms of life of the native people. The positive energy emanating from the different types of idols like the *pañcalohavigraha,* the *navabhāsanavigrahas, the dhvaja-stambhas,* etc. offer further scope for study in this direction.

References

1. E.B. Havell, *The Ancient and Medieval Architecture of India: A study of Indo-Aryan Civilization,* S. Chand, New Delhi, 1972, p 164; Also see Percy Brown, *Indian Architecture,* vol. 1, sixth reprint, D.B. Taraporevala, Bombay, 1971.
2. K.V. Soundara Rajan, *Indian Temple Styles,* Munshiram Manoharlal, New Delhi, 1972, p. 15.
3. Ibid., p. 6.
4. Geographically they represented three regions Aśva-krāntā, Ratha-krāntā and Viṣṇu-krāntā respectively each with 64 texts in vogue. cf. Jaya Sankar, *Temples of Kerala,* Directorate of Census Operations, Kerala, 1977, p. 24.

5. T.Madhava Menon (ed.), *A Handbook of Kerala,* vol. I, The International School of Dravidian Linguistics, Thiruvananthapuram, 2000, p. 251.
6. See Kanipayyur Damodaran Namboodiripad, *Tantrasamuccaya (Śilpabhagam)* (Mal.), Panchangam Pustakasala, Kunnamkulam, 9th edition, 2010.
7. Vide M.S. Sreedharan *Bharatiya Vigyan Manusha,* Publications Division of Government of India, New Delhi, 2005, p. 719.
8. Cheruvally Narayanan Namboordiri, *Thatchsastram Bhasha* Devalaya-vidhī, Devi Book, Kodungalloor, 2005.
9. P.G. Rajendran *Kshetravijnanakosam* (Mal.), D.C. Books, Thrissur, 2001.
10. Madhava Menon (ed.), op.cit., p. 243.
11. Jayasankar, op.cit., 1997, p. 44.
12. Ibid.
13. Kanipayyur Damodaran Namboodiripad, op.cit., p. 22.
14. M.S.Sreedharan, op.cit., p. 692.
15. Naduvattom Gopalakrishnan, *Keralacharitha dharakal* (Mal.), Maluban publications, Thiruvananthapuram, Second edition, 2010.
16. Cheruvally Narayanan Namboodiri, *Thatchusastran Bhasha* (Mal.) for details of the *Samuccayavidhi* for the divisions of the *garbhagṛha* and the specific parts for different deities. The original text published in the series Malayalam *Granthāvali,* no. 146, 1982/1157 – Based upon that Cheruvally Narayanan Namboodiri has brought out a freelance translation of *Thatchusastram Bhasha* (*Devālayavidhī*), Devi Book stall, Kodungalloor, 2005.
17. Ibid.
18. See for details *Kṣetravijñānakośam,* op.cit.
19. For details see *Tantrasamuccaya,* as well as Jayasankara, op.cit. Copies of the original palm leaf manuscript of the text are kept in Oriental Research Institute and Manuscripts Library, University of Kerala.

2

TRADITIONAL ARCHITECTURE IN KERALA: WITH SPECIAL REFERENCE TO 'NALUKETTU'

K. G. Sreelekha

India is considered to be the mother of *vāstu* as the ancient saints have formulated various principles of it. These were formulated thousands of years ago where the sages kept in their minds the result of sunlight and energy and stabilizing nature's five elements in such a way as to get the maximum advantage out of it.

Vāstu Śāstra, the refined combination of ancient Hindu traditions developed as an art, analyzed as a science and interpreted astrologically can lead the way in to healthy living. Basically Vāstu Śāstra deals with the exercise of architecture and building science and in fact it gives a fair touch in every aspects of life on the earth as well as the universe.

The art of arranging rooms and appliances in a house or building by following the divine laws of Vāstu is known as Vāstuvidyā. It will help to achieve success in various facets of life including family, professional, spiritual, financial, health and relationship. It also helps to bring peace and prosperity to home and its inmates.

Building a house as per the Vāstu norms is very much essential because it brings atmospheric natural energies. So constructing a house with the Vāstu principles will greatly bring peace, success and opulence to the dwellers residing in the house.

The architecture of Kerala has been influenced by Dravidian and Indian Vedic architectural science since over two millennia. The characteristic regional expression of Kerala's architecture results from the geographical, climatic and historic factors.

The *Tantrasamuccaya, Tacuśāstra, Viśvakarmīya, Mayamata, Manuṣyālayacandrikā, Mānavavāstulakṣaṇa, Devālayacandrikā, Bhāskarīyamatavyākhyā, Manuṣyālayalakṣaṇa, Vāstuvidyā,* and *Vāstulākṣaṇa* are the important architectural works which have a strong impact on Kerala's architectural style. The *Manuṣyālayacandrikā* a work devoted to domestic architecture is one such work which has its strong roots in Kerala.

The location feature of Kerala has influenced the social development and indirectly the style of construction. The evolution of domestic architecture of Kerala followed closely the trend of development in temple architecture. The primitive models were huts made of bamboo frame thatched with leaves in circular, square or rectangular plain shapes. The rectangular shape with a hipped roof appears to have been finally evolved from functional consideration. The closed form of Kerala houses were thus gradually evolved from technical considerations.

Types of Houses

A house in Kerala is generally called *Veedu.* The *veedu* gives shelter to joint-family of *tharavad.* The joint family system (*tharavad*-kinship system) consequently promotes the tradition of living in a huge shelter or mansion (*veedu*-object of house). The term is Dravidian and is used in some parts of Tamil Nadu and north Sri Lanka for all types of residential architecture, but generally the people of Kerala will refer to their *veedu* as *tharavad.* However, domestic architecture in Kerala is diverse. Particularly, tribal people have more ways of referring to house or huts according to locality, social status and structural types. Observations on the proper traditional house generated five types of spatial house structures.

There are five types of traditional domestic architecture or *Veedu* in Kerala, namely: 1. The humble house, unknown by any building treatise of Kerala, belongs to ordinary folk and tribal people *(cheri, chala, kudi, variyam or pisharam)*; 2. The *Ekaśālā,* an I-shaped single rectangular hall house, belongs to farmers or middle-class non-farmers; 3. the *Nalukettu,* a courtyard house, belongs to landlords; 4. The great mansion *Ettuketu* and *Patinarukettu* (double ettukettu) or much bigger structure, belongs to very rich landlords; 5. Commoner houses are simple ordinary houses scattered abundantly in the cities and villages. They still show applications of traditional construction and vocabulary in an eclectic popular and free manner.

Basically the domestic architecture of Kerala follows the style of detached building; row houses seen in other parts of India are not mentioned in Kerala except in settlements occupied by Tamil or Konkani Brahmins. In its most developed form the typical Kerala house is a courtyard type–*Nalukettu.* The central courtyard is an outdoor living space which may house some object of cult worship such as a raised bed for *Tulasithara* or *Mullathara.* The four halls enclosing the courtyard, identical to the *nalambalam* of the temple may be divided into several rooms for different activities such as cooking, dining, sleeping, studying, storage of grains, etc. Depending on the size and importance of the household the building may have one or two upper stories or further enclosed courtyard by repetition of the *Nalukettu* to form *Ettukettu* (eight halled building) or a cluster of such courtyards. Padippura, Poomugham, Chuttuverandah, Charupady, Ambalkulam, Nadumuttom, *Pūjā* room are the main elements of *Nalukettu.*

Nalukettu

Nalukettu is the traditional home of Tharavadu where many

generations of a matrilineal family lived. These types of buildings are typically found in the Indian state of Kerala. The traditional architecture is typically a rectangular structure where four blocks are joined together with a central courtyard open to the sky. The four halls on the sides are named *Vadakkini* (northern block), *Padinjattini* (western block), *Kizhakkini* (eastern block) and Thekkini (southern block). The architecture was especially catered to large families of the traditional *tharavad*, to live under one roof and enjoy the commonly owned facilities of the *marumakkathayam* homestead.

ELEMENTS OF NALUKETTU

1. *Padippura*

It is a structure containing a door forming part of the compound wall for the house with a tiled roof on top. It is the formal entry to the compound with the house. At present the door is not there as car will have to enter the house through the entry. Still tiled roof is provided preferably with a traditional type lamp below the roof. Instead of door for entry, we now have the gate.

2. *Poomukham*

It is the prime portico soon after steps to the house. Traditionally it has a slope tiled roof with pillars supporting roof, sides are open. In the earlier days, the head of the family called *Karanavar* used to sit here in a reclining chair with *thuppal kolambi* (Spittoon) by the side of chair. This chair will have long rails on either side where the *Karanavar* will keep his legs raised for comfortable rest.

3. *Chuttu Verandah*

From the *Poomukham,* a verandah to either side in front of the house through open passage called *Chuttu Verandah.* *Chuttu Verandah* will have hanging lights in equal distance hanging from its slope roof.

4. *Charupady*

By the side of *Chuttu verandah* and *poomukham*, wooden benches with carved decorative resting wooden pieces for resting the back are provided. This is called *Charupady*. Traditionally the family members or visitors used to sit in these *Charupady* to talk.

5. *Ambal Kulam (pond)*

At the end of *Chuttu Verandah* there used to be a small pond with rubble on sides where lotus or *Ambal* used to be planted. The water bodies are maintained to synthesize energy flow inside.

6. *Nadumuttom*

Traditionally *Nadumuttom* or central open courtyard is the prime centre of the *Nalukettu*. There is an open area usually square in the exact middle of the house dividing the house on its four sides. Due to this four side division of the house, the house has a Nadumuttaom. Similarly there was Ettukettu and Pathinarukettu which are quite rare with two and four Nadumuttom respectively. Nadumuttom will be normally open to sky allowing sunshine and rain to pour in. This is to allow natural energies to circulate within the house and allow positive vibrance within. A *tulasī* will be normally planted in the centre of Nadumuttom, which is used for worship. Architecturally the logic is to allow the tree to act as a natural air purifier.

7. *Pūjā Room*

Pūjā room should preferably be in the north-east corner of the house. Idols can be placed facing east or west and the person praying can face west or east respectively. At present, wooden paneling is done on *pūjā* room walls and there is a standard design for *pūjā* room which can be given to clients interested in having traditional *pūjā* room.

Key Features

The whole house is protected with a compound wall or fence. An entrance structure (*padippura*) may also be constructed like the *gopuram* of a temple. This may contain one or two rooms for guests or occasional visitors who are not entertained in the main house. The position and sizes of various buildings, including the location of trees and paths within the compound wall were to be decided from the analysis of the site according to the prescriptions in the classic texts. This analysis involved the concept of *vāstupuruṣa maṇḍala* wherein the site (*vāstu*) was divided into a number of grids (*padam*) occupied by different deities (*devatā*) and appropriate grids were chosen to house the suspicious structures. The site planning and building design were done by learned Viśvakarmā sthapatis (master builders) who synthesized the technical matters with astrological and mystical sciences. There are numerous buildings of the *Nalukettu* type in different parts of Kerala, though many of them are in a poor state of maintenance. Changing socio-economic conditions have split up the joint-family system centered around the large *Nalukettu.* The Kailasa mandiram at Kottakkal belonging to the Arya Vaidyasala is a standing example of a three storeyed *Nalukettu* complex. Of the best preserved examples of this type are Mattancherry Palace at Kochi and the Taikottaram of the Padmanabhapuram palace near Kanyakumari.

Nalukkettu type buildings are also seen in many villages and towns, occupied by prominent people. The humbler building of the population are however smaller and simpler in form but basically derived from the *Nalukettu. Nalukettu* is a combination of four halls along four cardinal directions, centered around the courtyard or *aṅgana* one may build any one of the four halls (*ekaśālā*), a combination of two (*dviśālā*) or a complex of three (*triśālā*) depending on the needs. The most commonly found type in Kerala is the *ekaśālā* facing east or north. Being located on the western and southern sides of the *aṅgana* they are referred to as western hall (*padinjattini*) and southern hall (*thekkini*) respectively.

Nalukettu can be differentiated based on structure occupants and by the number of floors. Traditionally *Nalukettu* has one courtyard; however some *Nalukettus* have two courtyards, which are known as *Ettukettu*. While *Nalukettu* and *Ettukettu* are more common, *Pathinarukettu* are extremely rare, due to its enormous size.

Ancient architecture of Kerala has a very distinctive style. It is an ensemble of simplicity and elegance, simple and all embracing; it is tailored to suite Kerala's climate and culture. Though much of its secrets have passed into history, the buildings still stand as testaments to the skill of the ancient builders.

3

THE SOCIAL CO-TEXT AND CONTEXT OF THE TRADITIONAL KERALA ARCHITECTURE

V. Rajeev

Kerala shelters a unique system of architecture, embedded in the beliefs, legends and rituals of the society from time immemorial. The traditional architecture of Kerala had a grand and scientific history of its own. The architecture of Kerala had its origins in temple architecture and traditional house modelling. Our Vāstu system was substantially influenced by a host of social and environmental factors such as geographical conditions, climatic peculiarities, availability of raw materials and social system. Among the social indicators, the prominent place goes to caste system, feudalism, practice of untouchabilty, rites and rituals, gender discriminations and agrarian mode of production. Among these prominent place should be given to caste system and gender inequality. The system of caste discrimination occupied a prominent place not only in the modelling of houses, but also in the process of naming it.

The economic relations prevalent in society always had a significant say in the manner and method of house construction. The elite/upper castes in the society built their homes under the nomenclatures like *Nalukettu, Ettukettu, and Pathinalukettu,* etc. Caste-based segregations commence from the very moment a piece of land is chosen for construction.

According to the position of landscape, it is divided into *Govīthi, Gajavīthi, Nāgavīthi* and *Dhānyavīthi,* etc. Only on the basis of caste hierarchy, people are permitted to select the land classified above. For example, land with slope in north direction is appropriate to the Brahmins, while as land slopping to southern direction is congenial to the Kshatriyas. (Nampoothiri Chennnas, 2010, pp. 11-13). But the pinciples of *vāstu* were not followed precisely in the construction of houses belonging to the lower class. Even in the selection of proper location for houses and measurements, the influence of caste is visible.

Kerala is supposed to be the land of Paraśurāma. So it is obligatory for the Brahmins to have kitchen in the northeast direction of the house. Kitchen, the most prominent part of a home, belongs to the category of sub-house (*Upagṛha*) and it is separated from the main structure of the house. The gender discrimination and the marginalization of women in Kerala society accounts for this phenomenon. The taboo put on being seen by men not belonging to the family and the marginalised condition of women influenced the positioning of the kitchen.

The well was near the kitchen or even inside the kitchen to prevent it from being contaminated by the touch of the lower caste. The front portico (*Poomukham*) is assigned to the patriarch of the house and the back portion called kitchen is usually given to women. It was the rule of the day. Even meals were taken in separated areas designated for men and for women. The position of the door and the bedroom also differed according to *Varṇa* (Narayanan Nampoothiri Cheruvally, Trans, pp. 42- 43). It is noted that the measurement scales used for each caste were different according to our traditional Vāstu. Accordingly the scales which were used for upper castes were not permitted to the lower castes. But the interesting fact is that the scales used for lower castes were permitted to upper castes with out any restrictions (Narayanan Nambuthiri, 2011, p.100).

Even in the carving of idols in temples, this practice of gender inequality prevails. The construction of a temple is strictly based on the concept of male (*Puruṣa Saṅkalpam*). According to *Puruṣa Saṅkalpam* the *Śrīkovil* is the head, *Antarāla* the face, *Ardhamaṇḍapa* the chest, *Dhvajastambha* the pennies and *Balipīṭha* the anus. The wood and stone meant for temple work is strictly restricted to male specimens alone. *Vāstu* texts elaborate the appropriate attributes of such wood and stone chosen. It can be seen that even in the selection of inanimate objects like stone and wood, gender discrimination was followed. The shape of *Śivaliṅga*, the idol of Lord Śiva was different for different *varṇas*. *Tantra-samuccaya*, the authoritative text on *Vāstu*, confirms all the facts mentioned above.

The agrarian system of Kerala too had influenced the structure of houses built. In the same way, the joint family system, man-woman relationship, concept of individual liberty, etc. determined considerably the structure of the house. Moreover, the practice of untouchability also had a crucial role. William Logan has noted that even in the names of habitats the influence of caste and gender is observed. Based on *varṇa*, houses were designated as *Mana, Illom, Bhavanam, Pura, Veedu, Kudi, Chala, Cheri*, etc. Houses could be given only male names like *Moolakkaran Veedu, Thalikkaran Veedu, Kollan Parambil, Vaanian Veettil*, etc. Houses were designed by Brahmins. The actual craftsmen were mere underlings who followed their instructions. Moreover the *Tantrasamuccaya* directs that the master or *Ācarya* of *vāstu* should belong to the Brahmin community only (*Guru vipra ashen*) (Chennas Nampoothiri, 2010, p. 4)

Metaphysical beliefs also played an important role in this. This includes the concepts of *Vāstupuruṣa*, the area of the house, the sacred paths (*vīthis*), *Brahmasūtra* and *Karṇasūtra*. In every household, certain sacred spaces are restricted to certain members on certain occasions. The central concept of *Vāstuvidiya* in the moulding of temples and houses is particularly based on the social structures of society. Equal importance were given to social realities like caste system, gender inequalities, etc. along with *vāstu* principles in the designing and building of houses and temples.

In this way this paper explores meticulously how the feudal mode of social relations had impact on the indigenous tradition of architecture in Kerala. Hence we can conclude that, like all other branches of informative literature the Vāstu tradition also was dedicated to the upper caste.

References

1. Thirumangalathu, Neelakandhan Moosad, *Manuṣyālayacandrikā,* Narayanan Nambuthiri [Translation], 2011, D.C. Books, Kottayam.
2. Chennas Nampoothiri, *Tantrasamuccaya,* vol. I: 1178- Mal, Panjamgam Pusthaka Sala, Kunnamkulam.
3. Cheruvalli Narayanan Nambuthiri [Translation], 2009, *Vāstuvidiyā* D.C. Books, Kottayam.

4

APPLICATION OF VĀSTUŚĀSTRA IN THE CONSTRUCTION OF TEMPLES AND HUMAN ABODES

PHILIP JOHN

The Science of Vāstu can broadly be identified as the Science of Architecture. The Science of Vāstu is as old as Vedic literature in India. 'Sthapatya Veda', an 'Upaveda' of Atharva Veda, is the very source of the Science of Vāstu (or Vāstuśāstra). Vāstu was one of the thirty-two sciences prevalent during the Vedic Period. Vāstu combines in it various streams of knowledge such as Mathematics, Astrology, Geology, etc.

The architecture evolved at a particular place is intimately connected with the history and culture of that locality. Thus different phases are identified in Indian Architecture, and these, in turn, correspond to the different administrative or cultural eras such as the Era of Indus Valley Civilization, the era of Aryan domination in South India, Mahajanapada period, the era of Magadha empire, the era of Maurya Empire, Śuṅga period, Śātavāhana Period, Kuṣāṇa period, Gupta Period, South Indian Royal period, Pāla-Sena Royal Period, Deccan Period etc. Together with these India has also Dravidic, Muslim, Western and Modern architectural traditions. Each of these has its own peculiar features. These architectural traditions have also been influenced greatly by the religious, cultural, economic and geographical compulsions of the respective period.

Archaeologists have unearthed from the sites of the Indus Valley civilization remnants of living abodes and allied constructions, religious edifices, other buildings, stone statues, etc. These bear ample witness to the architectural designs of the Indus Valley phase of our nation's cultural history.

The Buddha vihāras attest to the characteristic features of the architecture of the age of the Buddha. They testify to the systematically codified architectural patterns of the Buddha period. There are clear stipulations for the construction of pillars and columns. Palaces and sculptures are the major constructions and art of the Mauryan period. They also have pillars to their credit. The Suṅga period and the Śātavāhana era also have pillars of sorts.

The Kuṣāṇa era is noted for its mingling of religion and beauty in architecture. Even though foreign influence is discernible the Kuṣāṇa architecture is predominantly Indian in design and execution. We have so many statutes of gods and goddesses, and of human beings belonging to this period. Gāndhāra architecture also gives much importance to the making of statutes.

Gupta era concentrates on the construction of temples. Statutes brimming with divine consciousness are peculiar to this age. The age of the Pāla Sena Kings also is noted for the construction of temples, especially chariot like - temples. The Deccan era has so many famous cave-temples to its credit. The Cālukya kings are known for their patronage of cave-temple architecture.

The Drāviḍa architecture has been developed under the patronage of the Pallava, Chera, Chola, Pandya, Vijayanagara and Madura monarchs. There are so many temples, maṇḍapas and different types of buildings belonging to this age. Each era concentrates on the different aspects of the external elegance and internal beauty of the temples and other buildings. This period is also known for its variety in the field of construction.

Muslim architecture concentrates on the construction of beautiful edifices. Monuments are given precedence over temples during this period. But the western style that has followed the Muslim period gives importance to temples, palaces, human abodes and other buildings. Our Modern Architecture is a continuation of Western tradition.

Thus Indian architecture which has passed through different phases has not abandoned its ancient traditions. Moreover, Modern Indian Architecture makes deliberate attempts to return to the golden traditions of our glorious past.

Vāstu Architecture is today known as the art of 'house building'. For in the construction field, human abodes take precedence over temples and other buildings. Hence the Vāstu architecture is identified as the art of human abode construction. Specific and clear instructions have been given by each age regarding the construction of human abodes.

The project of house builiding is described in detail in the Vāstuśāstra: it begins with *ācārya-varaṇa* and proceeds to elaborate the roles and responsibilities of 'Sthapati', 'Sūtragrāhi', 'Takṣaka'and 'Vardhaṇki'. The selection of proper land and location is the next step. Tips are provided to ascertain the proper land where 'Śaṅku Śthāpana' (marking) is to be made. Instructions are also given to identify the directions (east, west, south, north) of the land, and where the abode is to be constructed. Means are also suggested to rectify the *gṛha doṣas* if any.

Vāstu also provides tips for identifying the characteristic features and various forms of human abodes. The forms of houses range from '*ekaśālā*' to '*catuḥśālā*' and their related wings. There are stipulations regarding the measurements of all sorts of houses, and their constituent parts like the floor, walls, etc. There are also stipulations regarding adjacent buildings (cattle shed, out house, '*padippura*', store, dining house, etc.), their measurements, location, etc. Vāstu also speaks about those trees to be planted near the abode and those to be avoided. It also speaks about the advantages of following their stipulations and the evil consequences if they are ignored.

Temple construction also follows the very same rules of abode construction. It also begins with '*ācārya-varaṇa*'. The ācārya then does 'Bhūparigraha' with the help of his co-celebrants. Following the rules of the Vāstuśāstra they identify the proper place, and begin the construction of the temple. The '*guṇas*' of the land selected for the construction of the temple are the same as those of the abode. The positive effects of the '*pratiṣṭhā*' depend upon the '*guṇas*' of the land chosen for the construction of the temple. Once the location is marked and '*bhūparigraha*' performed the basic stone can be laid. Out of '*yoni*', '*āyam*', 'vyayam', '*nakṣatra*', '*tithi*', '*vaya*' and 'ā*zhcha*' only the sublime can be selected. Construction of the floor and, if necessary, the errection of the '*upa-pīṭha*' are the next step. There are different forms and stipulations for the same. The construction of the '*garbhagṛha*' is very important. The '*pratiṣṭhā*' is to be performed for each deity at the proper place following the relevant stipulations.

There are specific prescriptions for the construction of outlets from the sanctum sanctorum. Their specific parts and their measurements are contemplated in the Vāstuśāstra. The construction of the pillars is also important. The different forms of the pillars, their different parts, and their measurements are stipulated in the Śāstra. There are specifications for the doors, walls, roof, dome, etc. The number of the storeys of the '*prāsādas*' and their measurements are also discussed in the Vāstuśāstra. The '*prāsādas*' are classified on the basis of the number of storeys and their measurements. They are also classified according to their shapes. Thus we can accept shapes like the circular, rectangular, '*gajapṛṣṭha*' '*dīrghavṛtta*' '*ṣaḍasra*' 'aṣṭāsra', etc. for the temples. The temples are named according to their shapes. The different parts of the '*prāsādas*' and their allied structures are to be constructed according to the stipulations of the Vāstuśāstra. The different forms and shapes, location and decoration of the allied structures from the light house to the '*dhvaja*' are also prescribed in the Vāstuśāstra.

We have already noted that the Science of Vāstu has described in detail the rules regarding the construction of human abodes and temples. If we compare the stipulations pertaining to the two types of constructions we can see that there are both similarities and differences.

In the construction of the temple the '*ācārya varaṇa*' is to be performed by the '*yajamāna*' while the head of the family does it in the case of the abode buildings.

In the case of the temple, the 'parikarmikas' also must be present with the '*yajamāna*' while '*ācārya varaṇa*' is performed, whereas the ācārya selects the architects for the construction of human abodes.The same *guṇas* of land are acceptable to both the temples and the human abodes. But there is a difference regarding the place selected for the construction of the temple and that of the human abode. It is necessary to identify the directions for the construction of both temples and abodes. Wrong direction is not suitable for either. The procedure to determine the direction is the same in both cases.

Śaṅkusthāpana is one of the initial ceremonies of both abode and temple construction. Usually only one *Śaṅku* is errected for the construction of an abode. It is erected at the south-west corner. The *Śaṅkus* must be collected from the sap trees. In Kerala they are gathered from jack trees. For the construction of the temple nine *Śaṅkus* are to be erected. And they must be collected from 'punna' tree.

Even though the floors usually contain different parts, it is not quite necessary in the case of human abodes. But it is absolutely necessary for the temples.

Circumferences (*bālya, kaumāra, yauvana, vārdhakya* and *maraṇa*) are very important in the construction of abodes and temples. External circumferences, internal circumferences and the circumference of *'upagṛhas'* are especially considered in the Vāstuśāstra. Even though all the circumferences except 'maraṇa'are acceptable, the measurements of the sublime circumferences alone are to be preferred.

Compared to the walls of human abodes, the walls of the temples are beautifully decorated. Usually the walls of the temple are not colourfully painted, but only whitewashed. If there are portraits they will be coloured.

As far as the doors of human abodes are concerned, strength is preferred to beauty. But it is inevitable to beautify the walls of the temple. Often metallic designs are inlaid on such doors. On the other hand, windows are given special attention as far as human abodes are concerned.

The roofs of both human abodes and temples have sufficient slope for the rain water to drain off easily and speedily. The roofs of human abodes are simple on the whole, but those of the temples are usually very complex.

The human abodes are constructed with one or more wings. With regard to the number of storeys both abodes and temples are alike. Multi-storeyed constructions are there in both cases.

Allied wings ('*upagṛhas*') are part of both human abodes and temples. Wells, ponds, trees, etc. are also attached to both.

In the temples together with the chief '*pratiṣṭhā*' there are sub '*pratiṣṭhās*' as well. In human abodes there are both '*paradevatā pratiṣṭhā*' and statues for daily *pūjās*. It is necessary that both of these should be imbued with divine consciousness.

Local peculiarities and differences are characteristic of human abodes. But they are not seen in the case of temples. The differences of caste and religion also affect the architectural style of human abodes. So also, depending on the installation of different idols of deities, the temples also admit different architectural designs.

5

VĀSTUŚĀSTRA FOR SUCCESS IN LIFE

DESIKOM REGHUNADHAN

Almost all people desire happiness and social upward mobility in life. The home you inhabit is as important as education, wealth and profession, especially in terms of life security. One's identity and status are directly linked with his home address. The space you live in may have different names like *gṛham, bhavanam, veedu, illam, matdam* and so on like home, house, villa, bungalow, mansion, palace, etc. And here comes the relevance of Vāstuśāstra, the traditional architectural science of India. You can make your home a tremendous source of energy both to the dwellers and the visitors, if you integrate the principles of Vāstu while making the building.

Homes can be built after assessing the positive and negative properties and energy levels of the place, and then reducing the negative forces and making use of the positive elements to its maximum extent, with the help of the Vāstuśāstra.

The proverb 'woman for wedding and land for building' indicates the significance of the terrain you intend to build your home. A baby is conceived in the minds of the parents before it takes physical form. Similarly, a lot of dreams, imagination and calculation must have been done before a plan is made and a home materialized. But everyone who makes houses may not have a clear idea of the Vāstuśāstra. A few have some idea about Vāstu. It is advisable that they consult with the experts in the field before they venture to build their homes. There is no doubt that they will only benefit from this.

The principles of Vāstu are based on *pañcabhūtas* (the five basic elements the cosmos is made up of—water, air, fire, sky and earth), weight and measurement. The ideal combination of *pañcabhūtas* brings in a magical harmony like the one we experience in *pañcavādya* where all the five musical instruments play together complementing each other. This helps to intensify the positive energy level at home. Weight too has an important role to play. The distribution of weight is a matter of serious consideration. If the weight exceeds at undesirable points in the house, its inmates' efforts to forge in life are bound to meet with failure like the kicking by a man with elephantiasis. Measurements also have to be well balanced and properly ordered. Space has to be used in correlation with its use. Too much space or too less space would not serve the purpose.

Home is like a human body. The body of nature, human being and other living things is the design of an unknown and supreme architect. What would have happened had our limbs been positioned differently? Not only that they would fail to perform their duties but that would create various inconveniences as well. Imagine that our eyes were placed at some other place in the body! Similarly, each part of the house is like a limb in our body. If a part is not in its proper position it would create total chaos. A home has both an external body and an internal ambience.

Weight also has similar impacts. A man may be able to carry 100 kilograms of weight on his head. But he won't be able to walk much farther if he carries it on some other part of his body. If you pay special attention to weight distribution while building the house, it will definitely bring good results. Directions like east, west, north, south too have great significance in the construction of a house. The house should be designed in such a way that directions having positive energy is maximized and the ones with negative energy minimized. The parts of the house in relation to their purposes must be situated in accordance with properties of the directions. When part of a house facing a certain direction is considered to be suitable for disposing of refuse including faeces, another direction is considered to be safe for the use of fire, water etc. A room built facing the wrong direction can cause trouble.

The smooth entrance and exit of energy through the house is a matter of vital importance. Sufficient light, water, air and the serenity of the terrain are also essential factors. Directions are related to life styles. At which direction the head has to be placed while lying down, from which direction the fire is to be lighted, the direction to which the toilet be placed—all such minute details must be taken care of.

If the bedroom, study, prayer room, kitchen, toilet, well, septic tank and every other part of the house are built in conformity with Vāstu rules regarding directions, it would be much healthier for the people who live in it. Main doors, side doors, windows, beams and pillars should also follow the same rules.

The lien of the land, its background, measurement, shape, environment and its liveliness are all key factors to be examined before starting the construction of the house. Even such minute details regarding the position of doorsteps and staircase to the placement of computers, washing machine and iron are clearly stated in the architectural science called Vāstu.

Plants, creepers and trees that can be grown around the house have also to be carefully chosen and planted following the rules regarding direction. Also there are clear instructions about where domestic birds and animals can be kept and where the parking space and doorsteps are to be located. Things that can be kept within the house, outside the house, the position of drainage, electric line, pipe line—Vāstu gives each and every detail about the construction of a house.

Houses too have certain *marmas* (highly sensitive and vital points in the body) as we have in our human body. They too have to be taken into consideration while building a house. They even include compound wall, gate and the surface of the land. The house should be in concordance with the configuration of Vāstu, *prathama* (primary), *dvitīya* (secondary) and *bāhya* (external) Vāstu.

Conclusion

Generally it is a natural instinct of living things to take refuge in some shelter at sunset after engaging in various activities during the day. What they seek is security and peace. When we look at the nests of various birds we come to realize that it is not only humans but all living beings wish to have a secure habitation. It is to this space they come back after finding food, take rest, share their happiness and sorrows, and mate for the survival of their species.

But for humans, apart from security and peace, house symbolizes the key to prosperity. Other living beings can only adapt to their environment. They still do not have the ability to change their surroundings.

Humans are endowed with superior intelligence and wisdom. With this faculty, man has always tried to shape nature to ensure his security. Man who used to find shelter on and under the trees, over the rocks, on plain ground, in caves and on meadows later began to make huts, cottages and mud houses using rocks, stones, sticks, mud and water. Now he constructs huge multi-storied buildings and is even planning to erect buildings in other planets.

The present Vāstuśāstra is the result of a close analysis of the history of habitation and its developments. Every culture in the world had its own way of determining the exact spot where the house is to be built and its construction methods.

In India, beginning from Varāhamihira, numerous sages have contributed to Vāstuśāstra. Vāstu is like different streams joining together to form a great river and there have always been experts in this field. Different schools of Vāstu were developed in India. But all of them had a single objective: to make a habitation from which man would benefit from nature and nature would benefit from man. In other words, neither should harm one another.

A home is also a place where procreation is done. So it is imperative that the house should in no way make any negative impact on the environment. The principle behind this is that those who build the house or their posterity should never suffer from the negative energy permeated from the environment. The chief intention is that generations after generation should be able to lead a healthy and prosperous life in that home.

Vāstu had been put to use in building palaces, temples, walls, forts, ponds, roads, villages and cities. This testifies that a house built according to the rules of Vāstu would empower its inhabitants. The approach of Indian Vāstuśāstra emphasizes that man and nature should maintain a complementary relationship, like mother and child. Man should fashion his habitation without disturbing nature.

As Kaṇva describes the love Śakuntalā cherishes for nature in the line "She never drinks water before watering you." Vāstuśāstra put forward an architectural science which teaches you to live in harmony with nature.

> "Living in a good home is
> Better than being in heaven
> Living in a bad house is
> Like being in a whirlpool."

6

THE TANTRIC EXPLANATION OF VĀSTU BASED ON "MAYAMATA"

MANOJ S. NAIR

The concept of *Vāstumaṇḍala and Vāstupuruṣa* is one of the basic theory on which the Vāstuśāstra is formulated on to its present form. Today many of those who practices Vāstu are totally ignorant about this basic concept and accept it as a decree from god without thinking of its true meaning. There is no doubt that all of our śāstras are derived out from thousands of years of Indian cultural and spiritual experience and from the higher state of minds of great saints. But even then all of these are built up on a strong background of philosophy. Each of the concepts or beliefs in the Vāstuśāstra stood on strong base of philosophy. Without understanding the philosophy one will never be able to use Vāstu principles in true form in its application level. Here in this paper I am trying to put forward a new finding for the basic concept of *Vāstupuruṣa* and *Vāstu-maṇḍala* on the basis of the Tantraśāstra.

One may wonder how "Tantra and Vāstu goes along?" but truly speaking many of the concepts in *Vāstuvidyā* are based on Tantra philosophy only. One can find the roots of both of these in *Atharvaveda.* Many of the ancient books on the Vāstuśāstra like the *Mayamata* etc. categorically put forward *pramāṇas* as as said by the *tantrikas.* In fact Tantra is another philosophy working on a higher state of mind which established the whole universe in a different pattern culminating in *Parā Śakti.* It is a philosophy which envisages doing some particular practices to attain self realization or "*moksha*" after fulfilling the desires in a dharmic way. It never denies worldly life. The Vāstuśāstra too provides a kind of surroundings for the inmates for slowly attaining self realization by adopting a successful worldly life based on dharma. All the rituals and *pūjās* in Vāstu is also Tantric. So the basic concepts adopted in Vāstu are strongly related with Tantra. My assumption is that one need to have a minimum knowledge about the Tantraśāstra for effective learning of the Vāstuvidyā.

Shape of Vāstumaṇḍala

As per the ancient Vāstu texts the *Vāstumaṇḍala* needs to be a direction-oriented largest square which can be inscribed in the plot. The size of the building, its facing, shape and dimension of the building must be based on this inscribed square. Many experts suggest that this *Vāstu manadala* can be triangular, circular or even rectangular, but I categorically negate this argument and assert once again that the *Vāstumaṇḍala* must be in a square shape. The philosophy behind this is from "Tantra". In the Tantraśāstra as well as in Tantric paintings earth is noted by a square shape only. No other shape is used to represent earth. In the physical plane too only the square shape can effectively represent the four cardinal directions: east, west, north and south. All other shapes create ambiguity in designing as all the mathematical proportions of perimeter *(chuttu)* used in Vāstu is based on the directions.

Segmentation of Vāstumaṇḍala

According to the *Mayamata,* the *Vāstumaṇḍala* can be segmented into smaller squares using one to thirty-two vertical as well as horizontal lines according to need for designing a village, a town or a building. This is also yet another theory based on the Tantra. The Tantra explains the whole of universe in thirty-six *tattvas* and out of that the thirty-first *tattva* is *māyā* and thirty-second *tattva* is *Śuddhavidyā.* So the *maṇḍala* too is divided on the basis of above theory. In *Śrīvidyā upāsanā* of ultimate Tantra, the Merucakra is represented with a square base and extends to a point in the tenth level showing attainment of *Tripurasundarī.* The square shows earth and the point (*bindu*) represents point of self realization which is the tenth level. On the basis of above theory, *maṇḍalas* segmented by 8, 9 and 10 vertical and horizontal lines are mostly considered for village planning, residential and temple designing respectively. Here 10 represents infinity or point of self-realization and 9 represents *māyā* which is the cause of our feeling of existence; 8 is further down level of solidity.

The concept of Vāstupuruṣa

The mythological story of *Vāstupuruṣa* is an excellent example of narrating a principle to an ignorant in a very effective way. The *Vāstupuruṣa* inside *Vāstumaṇḍala* lies with head towards north-east and limbs towards south-west. The east west central line is *Brahmasūtra* , north-south central line is *Yamasūtra,* north-east to south-west line is *Karṇasūtra* and south-east to northwest line is *Mṛtyusūtra.* In fact the line passing from north-east to south-west turns to be the central nerve passing from *mūlādhāra* to *sahasrāra* of *Vāstupuruṣa* as shown in the figure.

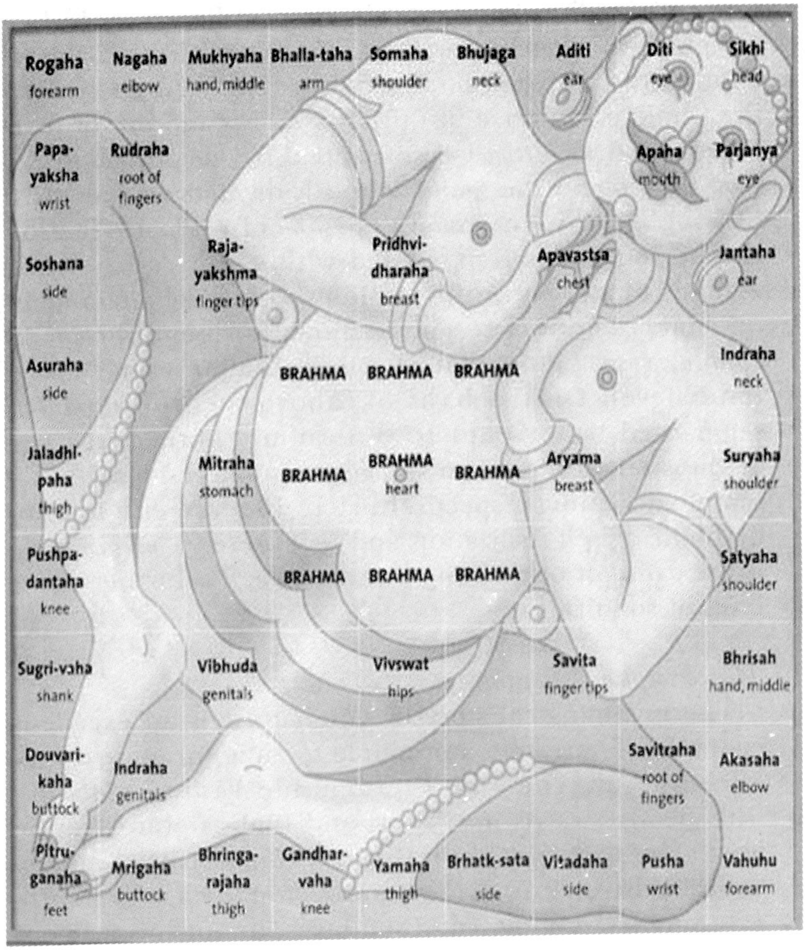

NORTH

The seven *cakras* as mentioned by Patañjali's *Yogaśāstra*

(1) Mūlādhāra
(2) Svādhiṣṭhāna
(3) Maṇipuraka
(4) Anāhata
(5) Viśuddha

(6) Ājñā
(7) Sahasrāra

can be identified on the *Karṇasūtra* of *Vāstumaṇḍala*. The most interesting thing to be noted is that the first signs of life generated between Mūlādhāra and Svādhiṣṭhāna in living beings, likewise the first vibration of generation of a structure will also be between *Mūlādhāra* and *Svādhiṣṭhāna* of *Vāstupuruṣa* which is in south western corner of *Vāstumaṇḍala*. So this can be one of the reasons for selecting south-west corner for *Svādhiṣṭhāna* (installation of first peg as well as place for foundation stone laying). The reason for selecting north-east or south-west sector of *Vāstumaṇḍala* for building construction is also the same. The major part of building needs to be located over the so called body of *Vāstupuruṣa*.

The 53 deities in and around the *Vāstumaṇḍala* may be representing different energy levels inside an independent *maṇḍala*. Each names of *devatā* as well as the area occupied by deities are easy way giving directions to the illiterate to design a building by allocating different rooms for different purposes. In this universe the basic constituent of all living and non-living beings is the same, so there is nothing wrong in comparing human body to a place where a shelter is being made to protect the same human body. This means that all the constituents in both cases may have similarity.

One more thing to be noticed is that, if you examine the names of *devatās,* those mentioned in the east side of *Vāstumaṇḍala* represents deities of Dawn and in the west reflects deities of Dusk. Deities on north show *devatās* of Birth and on the south reflects deities of Death. This shows that the *Vāstumaṇḍala* itself is a prototype of universe comprising of all activities in vicious universes.

THE SCIENCE OF VāSTU PURUṢA

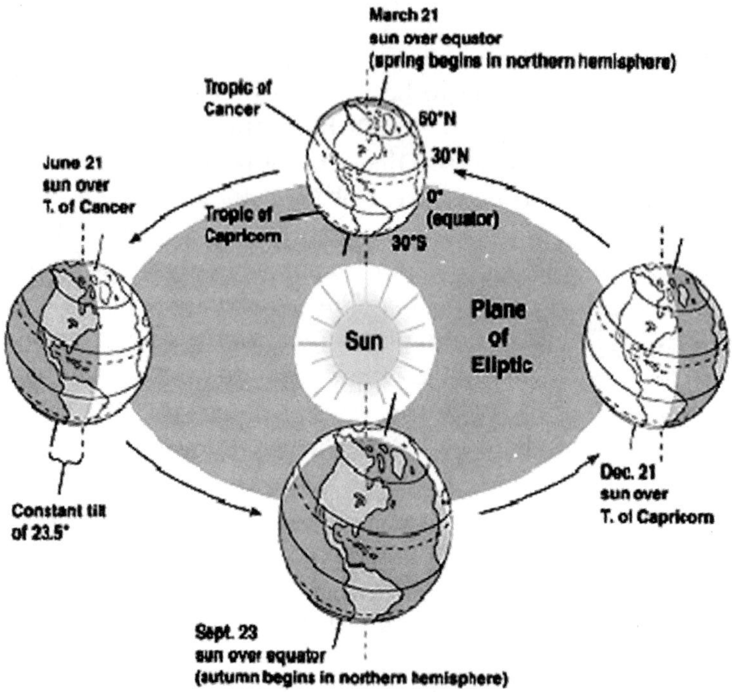

The mathematical proportions in *Vāstuvidyā* are being formulated on the basis of four directions, east, west, north and south. north-south, the direction of axis of earth, and east-west, the direction of revolution of earth. The only figure which can represent these features perfectly is square. This may be the reason of considering the *Vāstumaṇḍala* as the biggest square inscribed in a plot in main four cardinal directions.

The axis of earth may be created by a force which stabilizes the system of stars and which can be noted as pole star in modern science or as Dhruva star according to Hindu Astronomy. The lateral movement of earth around sun is the result of its the centrifugal and centripetal force.

The combination of these two may create a resultant force from southwest direction to northeast direction which can be called by the name *Karṇasūtra.* This axis of resultant energy becomes the backbone of *Vāstupuruṣa* and other powers (deities) stood over this conceptual figure. Through these explanations I would like to emphasize once again that *Vāstupuruṣa* is not simply a story or a pattern or a myth adopted for easy designing but it carries a lot of hidden *tattvas* in it. One more thing to be noticed is that in all cases related with Vāstu we need to consider true geographical north based on sun only rather than the magnetic north shown by compasses. The theory of magnetic field may not also evolved in those days of formulation of these theories.

Ultimately the Vāstuvidyā is a technic which is used by ancient India to condition the mind of humans by making certain arrangements in the physical plane he lives. The subtle changes Vāstu makes in life can be explained through the experience one attains by living there. It is a very difficult task to explain the theories under pure logic due to the vastness and depthness of its philosophy. The effectiveness of Vāstu, ultimately depends on the efficiency, intellectual capacity, spiritual discipline and calmness attained by the practioner and his grip over the philosophical background of Vāstuvidyā.

7

FEATURES OF DEVATĀPRATIMĀ (GOD'S IDOL IN THE TEMPLE) AS DESCRIBED IN THE MĀṬISADBHĀVA, A ŚĀKTA TREATISE OF KERALA

MACIEJ KARASINSKI

The term 'Tantra of Kerala' indicates a plethora of complex, interweaving ritualistic and speculative traditions. Kerala has been praised by scholars as a rich source of traditional knowledge domains. Yet, Tantric traditions of the State, with their voluminous scriptural data, still remain fairly unexplored by modern researchers. The Tantric canons preserve not only ritual peculiarities and philosophical ideologies but also deal with architectural details of sacred buildings and prescribe rules for preparation and consecration of idols worshipped in the Hindu temples. There is a common belief, cherished by the followers of Tantric cults, that while the transcendent form of a deity is unrealizable for a devotee one can worship the divine present in sacred images. Through a ceremony of installation and consecration, the images are transformed into receptacles of divine energies (*śaktis*). From the time of consecration the god is constantly present in his images. Indeed, an image (*pratimā*) becomes the god himself (*devatā*). Here one can quote a statement of B.C. Bhattacharya who declares that according to Hinduism, an icon is not only a representation of a deity but the image is meant for devotees who want to meditate on their chosen god (but are unable to visualize him mentally) and to become one with him.[1]

The aim of this paper is to remark on characteristic features of *devatāpratimā* (God's Idol in the temple) as indicated in a Tantric treatise entitled *Māṭīsadbhāva (MSB)*

MSB is a Tantric ritual handbook composed in all probability in *c.* 11th-15th centuries by unknown author who claimed to be well-versed in Śaiva and Śākta scriptures. The text has not been critically edited and is preserved in form of palm-leaf manuscript. The manuscript of *MSB* in Malayalam script is available in Trivandrum Manuscript Library (mss. no. 1017a, 13377). The importance of the data drawn from this source can be gauged from the distinctiveness of *MSB* as a rare example of Śākta text of Kerala. Therefore a study of the text can bring to light some details related to the unique styles of temple architecture in Kerala and construction or consecration of the idols. The present paper is based on the fourth chapter of *MSB* which deals with installation and features of *devatāpratimā*.

The text prescribes that images of gods should be prepared by experts (*śubha śilpin*) versed in iconography.[2] It is noteworthy that, according to the same passage, these artists ought to be skilled craftsmen who have studied architecture and are still young and careful [*śilpibhiś-śilpaśāstrajñair yuvadbhiścāpyatandritaiḥ (. . .)*]. In this respect it is worth to quote Vasudeva Poduval who states that most of sculptors of Kerala were artists, not merely carvers and their work was always marked by originality.[3]

MSB prescribes several materials that can be used for the production of idols.

Basically, an idol can be made of rock, clay, iron or wood.

aśmanā mṛttikābhirvā lohairvā dāruṇātha vā
dhātubhirvā prakartavyā devatāpratimā budhaiḥ/
(*MSB* 4.1)

Here it is only proper to cite Niharranjan Ray who states that according to Indian beliefs the material out of which sculptures are made (be it a boulder of stone, a lump of metal or a log of wood) is an object of a passive, inert matter, a part of organic scheme of things. Once it is cut out of natural ambiance it is no longer filled with primal, wild and everlasting energy that unites and sustains the human universe. However, the artist's own creative power can be set in the material and the image may be shaped according to the imagination of the craftsman.[3] Perhaps therefore one may suggest that the object uprooted from organic scheme of things is relocated by the artist in the divine scheme of things and it may reflect higher truths that are otherwise unattainable for ordinary humans.

According to *MSB* there are specific rules stating how to choose the proper material for an idol. Having decided what kind of material he may use, the wise man should wait till the proper time marked by all favorable signs. It should be a day of moon's increase (*śuklapakṣa*), a lucky hour blessed by auspicious star (*sumuhūrta sunakṣatra*). On that day the wise man should chant the 'bird-hymn' (probably *RV* I.164.20) in four quarters of the world and afterwards enter a forest with a solemn vow to find a proper material for an idol.

sumuhūrte sunakṣatre śuklapakṣe gurustadā
nimittaiśśobhanairgacched viprāśīrvacanaissaha
prācīṃ prāpyāthavodīcīmaiśānīmathavā diśām
japtvā śakunasūktantu praviśedvipinaṃ punaḥ
(*MSB* 4)

One should search thoroughly the surrounding area but, according to the text, there are places more auspicious than others (e.g. holy groves, banks of rivers or holy mountains) where an artist can locate the proper objects. There, one can find stones that are charming (*manojña*), one-coloured (*ekavarṇa*), smooth (*sama*), resplendent (*snigdha*), immersed in water (*saritsalilasambhūta*) and unmixed by other colors (*varṇabhedavivarjita*). All these above mentioned qualities are attributed to the best kind of stone that can be used by a craftsman. The stones are later classified into young, old and middle-aged (*śilā tu trividhā jñeyā bālā vṛddhā ca madhyamā*) and should necessarily be white, red, yellow or black in colour (*sitā raktā tathā pītā kṛṣṇā yathākramam*). Such meticulous taxonomies of building materials are indeed frequently found in Hindu literature that was later referred to by those who erected and consecrated temples in South India.[4]

If an idol should be made of wood, the text explains, one should search for particular trees. Indeed, the trees may be divided into castes (*caturṇāmapi varṇānāṃ vṛkṣabhedastvathocyate*). Hence, *Madhuka (Jonesia Aśoka), Candana (Sandal wood), Śrīvṛkṣa (Bilva tree), Śamī (Mimosa suma)* are considered as trees of the twice-borns or shall we say twice-borns among the trees. Obviously, there are certain trees that should never be cut down. *MSB* teaches that one should avoid trees that are burnt with fire (*agnidagdha*) or dried up (*śuṣka*). The craftsman must also check if the tree is inhabited by any supernatural being (*yakṣarakṣoniṣevita*) and if so, he should leave the place immediately. Trees growing near swamps or other damp areas should also be avoided. Once the choice is made, the wise man should clean the area and sprinkle it with sanctified water. Hereafter he may invoke Śiva and Gaṇeśa and ask them for help and benediction. Then he should prepare a fire ceremony. He must feed the sacrificial fire with various oblations and bless the area with protective spells and *piṅgala sūtra* (*agnikāryaṃ punaḥ kuryādbahurupeṣu mantravit kavacena piṅgalenaiva sūtra-kṛtvābhimantravit, MSB*, p.18). The rite should be followed by offerings for the tutelary deity (*kṣetrapāla*) and spirits living in the area. Having done so, one should stay one day at the place chanting proper mantra at night before falling asleep (*ekarātraṃ vasettatra svapnamantraṃ japettadā*). The mantra is given as: *namaśśāmbho trinetrāya piṅgalāya mahātmane vāmāya viśvarūpāya svapnādhipataye namaḥ.* The text states that one should remember his dreams that may occur during that night and a spiritual master may deliberate on their meanings afterwards. If any bad omen was seen in the nocturnal vision, additional offerings should be given to the deities (*svapne sarvāṇi kāryāṇi śubhānyapya-śubhāni ca tataḥ prabhāte vimale guruḥ svapnaṃ vicārayet śubhe siddhantyabhīṣmāṇi aśubhe homayecchatam MSB,* p.18). Only after that one can chop the tree and carry on with other preparations. The text continues to narrate various methods of preparing clay and finally constructing the idol (here called *bimba*) which should be filled with herbs and gems before the ritual of consecration is completed (*sarvavijñāni dhātūni ratnānyauṣadhayastadā bimbamadhye vinikṣipya vidhivatparikalpayet MSB,* p. 20). The idols, as described in the same chapter, can also be divided into several categories and should be conveniently measured by *aṅguṣṭha* (thumb's breadth) or *vitasti* (measure defined as a long span between the extended thumb and little finger). The text specifies the dimensions of idols giving detailed information on proportions and size of various details. Thus, even minor parts of sculptured bodies must have specific measurements, for example the proper size of ankles should be two *aṅgulas* and feet may not exceed the limit of fourteen *aṅgulas* (*vijñeyau dvyaṅgulau gulphau pādau caturdaśāṅgulau, MSB,* p.25). Similar instructions and rules are commonly found also in other Indian treatises on architecture. Thus, for example the prescribed features of holy idols are in agreement with traditional laws stating that an image should be smooth-jointed (*suśliṣṭasandhi*) and not showing any crossing of joints (*nigūḍha sandhikaraṇa*). There one can also find a general rule that the figure shall be portrayed in balanced pose; his or her apparel, ornaments and weapons must be harmonized with the bodily expressions.[5] It is clear from the general descriptions found in *MSB* that it was of utmost importance for an artist to translate the religious and mythological concepts into worshipable figures.

MSB states that the main image may be placed on pedestal (*sthaṣṇila*) with representations of various groups of divine or semi-divine beings (*gaṇā bhūtāstathā hrasvāstundilā bṛhadānanāḥ rākṣasā bhīṣaṇākārāḥ karālāḥ parikīrtitāḥ MSB,* p. 25). As mentioned by Vasudeva Poduval, the elegant images of gods found in temples of Kerala have significant aura of vitality and at the same time they possess distinguishable poise and grace.[6] J.H. Cousins added that the sculptures of Travancore can be called realistic (in the sense of the term as used in Western iconography); but, on the other hand, they are mystical because of their "tangible expression of intangible ideas."[7]

It is only in the subsequent chapter of *MSB* that the general remarks on iconography and preparatory techniques are supplemented by a detailed description of a goddess image, the one known as a solitary heroine (*athaikavīrīṃ pratimāṃ pravakṣyāmi samāsataḥ, MSB,* p.26). While in the fourth chapter we could find detailed explanations of preparatory actions, classification of materials, and measurements of images, the fifth chapter gives us a vivid and poetical description of the goddess, as she should be imagined and represented. The divine heroine is the one who killed a demon Ruru, a general of Dāruka's army and the legend about her exploits is summarized in chapter nineteenth of *MSB.* Moreover, the great battle between the goddess and demons is also alluded in *Brahmayāmala* text which again is frequently referred to by the author of *MSB.* The text (i.e. *MSB*) warns that only a dedicated adept who is an expert of mantras can perform rituals related to the goddess cult. In case of goddess who is called the slayer of Ruru there are serious dangers for a person who wants even to contemplate on her image. In fifth chapter of *MSB* we read:

evaṃrūpā jagaddhātrī nipātya rurudānavaṃ
bhītvā śūlena hṛdayaṃ mukhe tasyārpitekṣaṇā/
na kuryādūrdhvadṛṣṭiśca nādhodṛṣṭiśca deśikaḥ//
ūrdhvadṛṣṭyā bhavennāśamadhodṛṣṭyā bhayaḥ bhavet/
samadṛṣṭyā bhavenmṛtyustasmāttatparivarjayet//
MSB 5th chapter.

In this form the mother of the world having killed Ruru the Dānava, having pierced his heart with a spear, the guru having fixed his eyes on her face should not look upwards or downwards. If he looks upwards he will be destroyed if he looks downwards he will be scared. If he looks on the whole scene equally he will die, thus he should avoid that.

In later passages of *MSB* one can find similar dramatic descriptions of the goddess who is frequently called a lonely warrior queen.

dārukasya vināśārthaṃ nirmita viśvamūrtinā
maheśvaralalāme tu ekavīrī vinirgatā
pralayāmbudanirghoṣā pralayānalavarcasā
pralayānilavegā ca mahāmāyā parāparā
kṣaṇena dārukaṇ hatvā kiṃ brūhi vada śaṅkara

Having many forms, created to vanquish the demon Dāruka a solitary heroine who came out of the head of the mighty god (being) the sound of the clouds of destruction, the lustre of the fire of destruction, the vehemence of the wind of destruction, higher and lower (force) of the great illusion (*māyā*) having killed Dāruka in an instant what then? Tell (us) O Śaṅkara!

The text portrays the goddess as a fierce lady of dark complexion, even darker than storm clouds (*Kālñī vrīlitakālameghanivahair varṇena*). She is invincible, agitated by anger (*roṣoddiptā*); but on the other hand she is also a compassionate mother who protects her devotees and heals their distress (*duḥkhaharā*). She is always gracious (*satata bhadrā*) but she is also praised as Mahābhairavī: a formidable heroine who holds a club, a trident and a sword in her hands (*khaṭvāṅgatriśikhānasiṃca dadhatīṃ vande mahābhairavīṃ MSB*, p.27). The poetical stanzas concluded by prayers and benedictions supply a craftsman with detailed instructions on the construction of the image of the goddess. However, the artist has a considerable freedom of composing the whole idol according to his vision and to induce a flavor of originality into his work. Thus, for example, the terrifying image of the goddess can also indicate her inner power of creativity, the evident passion and willingness to lead the devotees to salvation at any cost. Such ambiguities of the divine characters may be reflected in the artistic form. The images of the goddess who killed Ruru and Daruka can be seen in the temples of northern Kerala: in Māmayikkāvu, Kalarivammukal or Nileśvaram. There one can notice how these poetic expressions of devotion found in Tantric texts were translated into the realm of iconography.

The chapters of *MSB* summarized here give us examples of rules and laws for preparation of idols. One should remember that the text is not an opus devoted to iconography only but a Tantric manual dealing mainly with ritual matters. However, even in a Tantric handbook one can find interesting stanzas on idol making. While reading one can find in the text a curious tension between strict rules of iconography and the call for an artistic freedom to fashion the idol according to his imagination.

Let us conclude with a quotation from Rene Guenon who once remarked that:

> Humanity attempts to embody in a tangible or otherwise perceptible form, we may say to materialize, what is in itself intangible and imperceptible. It makes symbols, written characters, and cult of images of earthly substance and sees in and through them the spiritual and divine

substance that has no likeness and could not otherwise be seen.

(Rene Guenon, *Du Pretendu Emprisme des anciens, Le voile d'ḍsis,* CLXXV, 1934)

Bibliography

Cousins H., 'The Art and Symbolism of Travancore Wood-carving', in: *The Arts and Crafts of Travancore.* ed. Stella Kramrisch, Trivandrum.

Coomaraswamy selected papers, ed. Roger Lipsey, Princeton University Press, 1977.

Rene Guenon, *Du Pretendu Emprisme des anciens, Le voile d'ḍsis,* CLXXV, 1934.

Radhakamal Mukerjee, *Cosmic Art of India,* Delhi, 1965.

Ravi Varma, 'Rituals of Worship', in *The Cultural Heritage of India,* 4: 453, quoted in: Gilles Tarabout, *Theology as History Divine Images, Imagination, and Rituals in India,* Vancouver, 2004.

Vasudeva Poduval, 'Sculpture in Travancore', in: *The Arts and Crafts of Travancore.* ed. Stella Kramrisch, Trivandrum.

Gilles Tarabout, *Theology as History Divine Images, Imagination, and Rituals in India,* Vancouver, 2004.

K. Vaidyanathan, *History of Vaishnavism in South India before Sankara,* Tirupati, 2002.

Mātīsadbhgva—mss. no. 1017a, 13377 Trivandrum Ravi Varma, 'Rituals of Worship', in: *The Cultural Heritage of India,* 4: 453, quoted in Gilles Tarabout, *Theology as History Divine Images, Imagination, and Rituals in India,* Vancouver, 2004, pp. 58–59.

References

1. (. . .) *in case of another Sanskrit word śubha of which the later meaning is 'lovely' there may be cited the expression śubha śilpin from the Rāmāyaṇa where the reference is certainly not to a craftsman personally 'handsome' but*

to 'a fine craftsman', Coomaraswamy selected papers, ed. Roger Lipsey, Princeton University Press, 1977, p. 247.

2. Vasudeva Poduval, 'Sculpture in Travancore', in: *The arts and crafts of Travancore,* ed. Stella Kramrisch, p. 47.
3. Niharranjan Ray, *Idea and Image in Indian Art,* Delhi, 1973, p. 59.
4. K. Vaidyanathan, *History of Vaishnavism in South India before Sankara,* Tirupati, 2002, p. 179.
5. Radhakamal Mukerjee, *Cosmic Art of India,* Delhi, 1965, pp. 54–58.
6. Vasudeva Poduval, 'Sculpture in Travancore', in: *The arts and crafts of Travancore,* ed. Stella Kramrisch, p. 47.
7. J.H. Cousins, 'The Art and Symbolism of Travancore Wood-carving,' in: *The Arts and Crafts of Travancore,* ed. Stella Kramrisch, p.116.

8

KERALA TEMPLES—A SPLENDOUR IN TIMBER ARCHITECTURE

Sheeja K.P.

Temples or *prāsādas* are abodes of gods, built of durable materials, which impart happiness to human beings. Timber has been used as a building material since the Vedic period. Kerala is rich and abundant in timber and temples of Kerala are a treasury of elaborate and intrinsic wood carvings. It is seen that structural temples in Kerala originated in the early years of the ninth century as per evidence. Temple architecture has experienced a series of development both in form and in interiors through the years. The development in wood carvings had reached its zenith in the late phase. Concentrations of wooden temples are mostly in the districts of Alleppey and Kottayam. Temples like Kaviyur Śiva Temple, Kandiyur Śiva Temple, Mahadeva and Narasimha temple at Chengannur, Kuttanperur Karthiyaini Temple, Śiva Temple at Vazhapalli, Ettumanur and Vaikom showed extensive works in wood. In such temples even walls are made of timber, bearing beautifully carved panels devoted to various epic and puranic themes. But the *adhiṣṭhānas* are built invariably of granite mouldings. The roofs are made of timber although some times covered with copper sheets which must have constituted an important item of import in the Kerala's maritime trade. Generally, the copper sheets have been nailed with the timber built roofs, obviously to protect the joints and stop leakage of rain water. The roof construction technique followed is not the same throughout. Sometimes tiles were spread over a wooden frame, the constructional method of which has been dealt with in the various Śilpa-texts like the *Tantrasamuccaya.* Bricks did not gain popularity in Kerala temple construction largely because of the easy availability of blocks of laterite and timber.

Classical sources of temple design

The classical treatise in temple construction in Kerala are the *Tantrasamuccaya* by Cennas Manakkal Narayanan Namputirippad (15th century) and *Śilparatna* compiled from the ancient Śilpa and Āgama works by Śrīkumāra' (16th century). The *Tantrasamuccaya* is in 12 paṭalas and the Śilpabhāga speaks about the temple construction. The text *Śilparatna* is divided into two parts—the first part consisting of 46 chapters on the construction of houses and villages along with other subjects and second part consisting of 35 chapters on iconography and related topics. Also important are *Mānasāra, Mayamata, Īśānaśivagurudevapad-dhati,* and *Prayogamañjarī,* and *Tantraratnavali.* The chapter 56 of the *Bṛhatsaṃhitā* Varāhamihira (6th century)deals with the *prāsādalakṣana* and treatment of temple architecture. The *Thachuśāstra* defines the temple layout and ritual procedures.

Temple design principles

The classic temple known as Ambalam or Kshetram or Tali has a Śrīkovil as its nucleus. The Śrīkovil may be round, square, rectangular, elliptical or apsidal. The temple normally faces the east. The structure above the *adhiṣṭhāna* (from plinth to spire) is called the *Vimāna.* Some structures are small and single storeyed namely *Ekatala* which is most popular. There are even two-storeyed and three-storeyed structures called *Dvitala* and *Tritala.* The upper levels of the Śrīkovil are not functional, but their role is to give a visual dominance. Temples are designated as *alpaprāsāda* and *mahāprāsādas.* Temples up to three storeys and the width up to 16 H is said to be *alpaprāsādas* and structures more than three storeys and width up to 64 H is called *mahāprāsādas.* (One Hasta H=24 aṅgula, one aṅgula is standardized as 3 centimeters).

The five-fold classification of temples according to the breadth-height proportions are: 1.*Śāntika,* where height = breadth; 2. *Pauṣṭika* (height=1.25 breadth); 3. *Jayada* (height = 1.5 breadth); 4. *Sarvakāmika* (height = 1.75 breadth); 5. *Adbhuta* (height = twice breadth). The height is divided into different ratios for *adiṣṭhāna, stambha, prastara, grīva, śikhara and stupi* for the five temples. The *vimānas* are classified as Nāgara, Drāviḍa and Vesara. According to the *Mānasara, Nāgara* vimana is square in shape from base to śikhara. The Drāviḍa vimāna has a polygonal shape from base to finial and *Vesara* has circular, elliptical and oval shapes throughout.

According to the *Matsyapurāṇa* the primary shape of the *prāsāda* has a 4x4 grid division resulting in 16 squares. The four cells in the centre form the *garbhagṛha* and the outer cell form the wall (*bhitti*).This forms the *Nirandhara prāsāda.* In *Sāndtara prāsāda* plan there exists an ambulatory passage between the inner walls (*khaṇḍubhitti*) and outerwall (*bāhyabhitti*) of the *garbhagṛha.* The *Pancaprākāra,* form five successive regions around the shrine, i.e.1.*antarmaṇḍala,* 2.*antahara,* 3.*madhyahara,* 4. *bāhyahara,* and 5. *maryādā.* These regions are marked with the width of the *prāsāda* as the unit measure (daṇḍa).The generally accepted measures are , 1, 1, 2, 4 and 7 daṇḍa from the outer side of the *prāsāda.*

Timber framed roof construction is categorised into three, i.e. *koṣṭha, śālā* and *sabhā.* Koṣṭha is a pyramidal or conical roof made of rafters resting on the wall plate and joining on a *kūṭa* at the top. *Śālā* is a gable ended roof. Here the rafter ends are supported on the wall plates at the lower end and the ridge at the top. *Sabhā* roof is a space frame provided for rectangular rooms. It is a combination of *koṣṭha* and *śālā.*

Evolution of Kerala temples

Kerala temples show a distinctive style which is largely an adaptation of the Dravidian style. The style is evolved by the influence of various geographical factors like the high precipitation, existence of dense forests and laterite formation. The political, economic and cultural factors of region has also influenced the evolution of the Kerala temple architecture. The political revival of the Cheras in the 9th century or even earlier coupled with the Bhakti movement provided a great fillip to the building of temples. Kerala temples were square, circular, rectangular, elliptical and apsidal in plan. The circular shrine has adapted certain features common in Northern India and Sri Lanka. According to the *Bṛhatsaṁhitā* in the north (6thcentury), circular temples constitute an important group. The apsidal plan of the temples in Kerala is imbibed indirectly from Andhra and Karnataka and these trends came to Kerala only through Tulunadu which has the highest number of apsidal shrines. Some of the apsidal shrines in Kerala have columns all along the circumambulated passage and the entire arrangement is reminiscent of the Buddhist architecture. The Kerala temples in the middle phase represented an amalgam of two styles- Dravida and Kerala. From outside it is a Kerala temple concealing in its core a small *Drāviḍa vimāna* having its own *grīva* and *śikhara* .The circular temple with a miniature *Drāviḍa vimāna* in the centre, the latter enclosed by one or two rows of columns may be compared with the circular Buddhist temple of Sri Lanka known as *Vatadage.*

The Kerala temple architecture is divided into three phases: Early (800 AD-1000 AD), Middle (1001 AD-1301 AD) and Late (1301 AD-1800 AD) according to H. Sarkar. Each phase shows an architectural evolution which is simpler at the beginning and becomes more and more elaborate later.

In the early phase the sculptural content was very less. But in the late phase the decorative and the visual arts like wood carving and paintings became prominent.

Early phase

The temples of the early phase were square, circular and apsidal in plan. Both *nirantara* and *sāntara* temples were in vogue. As a part of decoration recesses and projections were used. The typical layout of this phase consists of sanctum which may or may not be fronted by a *namaskāra maṇḍapa* and by a cloister enclosure known as the *nalambalam.* In square temples a small *mukha-maṇḍapa* projects from the larger sanctum. In apsidal and circular temples the space in front acts as a *mukha-maṇḍapa.* Kaviyur Śiva temple, Kandiyur Śiva Temple, Ettumanoor Śiva Temple etc. are examples of temples belonging to the early phase.

Middle phase

The temple architecture of Kerala in the middle phase showed developments in the interior arrangement. The temples were square, circular, apsidal and rectangular in plan .The elliptical plan was also in vogue. Many temples of this phase reveal the fusion of Drāviḍa and Kerala style. Another feature of this phase is the presence of more than one *pradakṣiṇa patha* around the *Garbhagṛha.* In circular and apsidal temples row or rows of columns run along the ambulatory. This concept is absent in square plan. The inner shrine of the circular temple is square in plan both internally and externally. In square temples the *Garbhagṛha* is square and in apsidal temples the *Garbhagṛha* is apsidal (*pṛṣtha*). The practice of raising the square shrine over a solid platform and approached by a long flight of steps came into existance. The Madathilappan Temple at Pervanam is an example of this type. *Tritala vimāna* also came into existence. In this phase, as in the early phase the placing of the detached *maṇḍapa* did not constitute an essential feature. The number of doors for the shrine was reduced to two or three and the concept of *ghana-dvāras* came into practice which is an interesting development noticed. Another additional feature of this phase is the practice of placing a *bhūta* figure below the *praṇāla*. Graceful figures of *dvārapālas* are datable to this phase.

Late phase

The temple architecture of Kerala reached its final stage of evolution both in dimensions and in exterior decorations during this phase. Majority of the temples were developed in this phase. Very little development has taken place in the general plan of the individual shrines but the layout of the entire complex has grown into greater elaboration and complexity. Sculptural art and ornamentation became elaborate which proved to be the period of Kerala's prosperity. The ideal organization of Kerala temple is by the *pañcaprākāra* of five successive enclosures ie. 1. *antar-maṇḍala,* 2. *antahara* 3. *madhyahara* 4. *bāhyahara* and 5. *maryādā.* The layout of the typical Kerala temple is shown in (Figure 1).The central shrine, the *Garbhagṛha* is fronted by a square *namaskāra maṇḍapa* with a square superstructure. In some temples, another pillared structure namely the *Balikal maṇḍapa* in front of the *valiambalam,* a wing of the *Nalambalam* provides the main entrance into the temple. *Kootamabalam* was also another addition. In larger temples the outer *prākāra* enclosed the temple tank. Decorative elements like *toraṇas* were in vogue. The *Sāntara vimānas* with one or more *pradakṣiṇa patha* dominated the temple architecture. Temples of this phase are square, circular (fig.2), apsidal, rectangular and elliptical in plan. The Śiva Temple at Vaikkom, exhibits an elliptical shrine with elaborate interiors. Wooden temples with minute carvings from epics and Purāṇas (fig. 3) came into existence in districts of Kottayam and Alleppey. This minute ornamentation of sculptures of Kerala resembles the Hoysala tradition of Karnataka. The emergence of multi-shrined complexes was the result of the Bhakti movement. *Tritala vimānas* were in vogue.

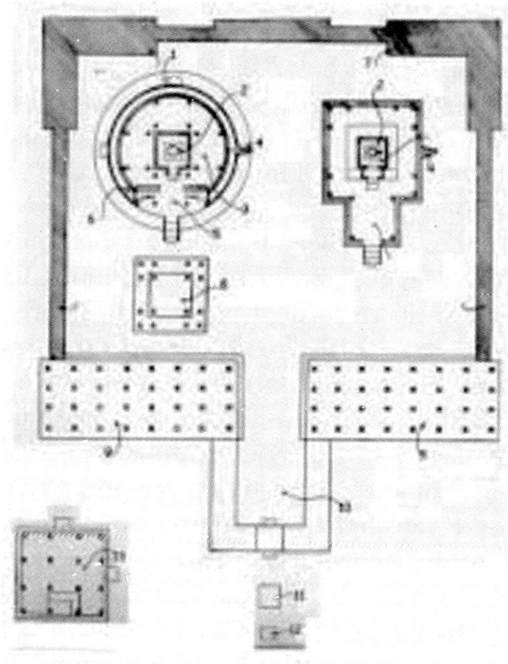

Fig. 1: Temple layout of Kerala

1. Vilaku madam	8. Namaskāra maṇḍapa
2. Antarāmaṇḍala	9. Dvāra gopura
3. Antahara	10. Agra maṇḍapa
4. Praṇāla	11. Balipīṭha
5. Mukhamaṇḍapa	12. Dhvajastambha
6. Sandhara(Ambulatory)	13. Koothambalam
7. Surrambalam	

Timber in temple construction

There are timber buildings in Kerala which has stood for more than 400 years. R.V. Poduval has stated that the wood work of the Śiva Temple at Katinamkulam near Murukumpuzha belongs to Kollam era 389 (1214 AD). Timber has a quality to span spaces. The width of the lintel of the door was taken as the key measurement and a kind of module in Kerala architecture. Timber may be classified into four categories according to ancient texts as *Antassāra,* with hardwood core (jack tree); *Bahissāra,* with hardwood outside (palm); *Sarvasāra,* hardwood all through (teak); and *Nissāra,* with softwood (Muringa). In the classical text *Śilparatna,* trees rejected for the construction purpose has been mentioned. They are those attacked by insects; have climbing creepers or bear thorns. Lumber should not be taken from trees that are used by Brahmins for worship; always bears fruits or located in the temple precincts. Also the trees standing by the roadside and the graveyard is to be avoided. Trees which are bent, dry and occupied by serpents, oozing water, producing milky sap, uprooted by wind or damaged by fire, trees growing in lakes and wells or at locations that are the meeting place of the rivers with the sea are to be rejected. Similarly trees pierced by the tusks of elephant, struck by lightning are to be rejected. But it is interesting to note that several restricted types like trees with milky sap may be used to build temples. Mixing of many species of wood in a structure is not desirable. The *Śilparatna* lists the following types suitable for dwellings: Saka (tectona grandis), Asana (terminalia tomentosa), Madhuka (bassia latifolia), Sala (artocarpus locucha), Sarja (vatica robusta), Candana (sandal sirium myritifolium), Panasa (jack tree or artocarpus heterophyllus) and Devadaru (avaria longifolia).The tree has to be felled in the evening (Viṣṇu-dharmottara).The temple is an image of the microcosm, as shaped from the primordial wood which is Brahman (Stella Kramrisch).The four members of the builder's guild, are *Sthapati* (master builder), *Sūtragrāhin* (cord-bearer), *Varādhaki* who increases (vṛdh) by joining together-stone craftsman and *Takṣaka* (carpenter). Takṣaka is one who reduces (*taks*) large pieces into small parts. He is stated to know the Veda and be skilled in his craft of wood joinery

(*Mānasāra*).The text also discusses on the properties of wood and its collection. Trees can be classified into male, female and neuter. The male tree has a uniform trunk width from base to top and without branches and gives cool shade with a pleasant form. The female tree has a pleasant form and provides shade and has a thick base which tapers to the top. The tree is neuter when its trunk is thinner at the base than at the top and does not provide shade. Wood that is male and female may be joined to the same or opposite gender. Neither male nor female may ever be joined to the neuter. The felling of the tree is done during the waning phase of the moon.

Kaviyur Śiva Temple

The Śiva Temple at Kaviyur in Tiruvalla taluk in Alleppey district has a circular structure, built of timber on granite *adhiṣṭhāna.* The temple has faced several alterations and the *adhiṣṭhāna* has survived which can be placed in the early phase. From the inscriptions on the *adhiṣṭhāna* it is evident that the temple must have come into being in the middle of the tenth century. The dates engraved on the Kumuda and Kapota are 4051(AD 950) and 4052 (AD 951).

The temple has a *vṛtta* (circular) *vimāna* enclosing a square *Garbhagṛha.* It has an *Ekatala vimāna.* The diameter of the temple is 10.86 m. The *Garbhagṛha* is surrounded by double *pradakṣiṇa pathas.* The temple is *Sāntara* type with eight columns in the ambulatory. The circular outer wall made of timber has four openings in the cardinal direction like the Sarvatobhadra type of temple. The *Garbhagṛha has* splendid and excellent wood carvings. Each intricate carving depicts an episode from the Purāṇas.

Sattankulankarai Narasiṃha Murthy Temple

The Sattankulankarai Narasiṃha Murthy temple in Chengannur taluk in Alleppey district, facing the west is built mainly of wood and it has a *sama-caturasra kṣudra-*

vimāna with a *namaskāra-maṇḍapa* in front. It is standing on a *mañca* type of *adhiṣṭhāna*. The *Garbhagṛha* has a roof covered with copper. The temple consists of a square *vimāna* enclosing a square *Garbhagṛha* (figure. 2) with a *pradakṣiṇa patha* all around. At each of the four corners of the *Garbha-gṛha* is a column. The *Garbhagṛha* too has its own entrance. The *adhiṣṭhāna* of the outer wall (*bāhyabhitti*) is also of granite, and the mouldings comprise Upana, a short Jagati, Vṛtta Kumuda, Kaṇṭha with Siṃha mālā and Paṭṭika. Above it comes the *vedikā* followed by *bhitti.* This wall is made of wood and it is carved beautifully with various puranic scenes. There are *jāli*-windows (figure. 3), *devakoṣṭhas* and animal friezes on the wall. Above the *vedikā* runs a frieze of animal procession followed by another horizontal frieze of *vimāna* motifs. The temple has four functional doors, each one associated with *dvārapālas.* The carvings on the wall are excellent piece of art showing minute details of the various scenes from Kṛṣṇa līlā, Setubandhana, Putanā- vadha etc. Below the functional door of the northern wall is placed the Praṇāla. It is held in the *siṃha's* mouth. The Prastāra of the temple is highly ornate. This is undoubtedly a store house of sculptural art in wood. Considering the stylistic features these reliefs may however be dated to the fifteenth century when the temple in the present form came into existence.

Fig. 2 : Square Garbhagṛha

Fig. 3 : Jāli window

Fig. 4 : Circular Śrīkovil-praṇāla

Fig. 5 : Wooden Panels with carvings

Conclusion

The temple architecture of Kerala is remarkable for its simplicity. The *Garbhagṛha* has splendid and excellent wood carvings. Each intricate carving depicts an episode from the Purāṇas. This wall is made of wood and it is carved beautifully with various puranic scenes. There are *jāli*-windows, *devakoṣṭhas* and animal friezes on the wall. Above the *Vedikā* runs a frieze of animal procession followed by another horizontal frieze of *vimāna* motifs. The temple has four functional doors, each one associated with *dvārapālas*. The carvings on the wall are excellent piece of art showing minute details of the various scenes from Krishna līlā, Setubandhana, Śiva Pārvatī etc. The *Prastāra* of the temple is highly ornate. This is undoubtedly a store house of sculptural art in wood. Technically the most important feature of temple architecture is the planning and design principles using dimensional standardization. The dimensional coordination up to the minute construction detail and the explicit wood work makes Kerala temple a unique marvel.

Bibliography

1. Cennas Manakkal Narayanan Namputirippad, *Tantrasamuccaya.*
2. T.Ganapati Sastri (1922). *Śilparatna.*
3. Jose Jacob (ed.) (2003).*The Architectural Theory of the Mānasāra,*Thesis. Mc Gill University, Montreal.
4. Balagopal T.S. Prabhu, A. Achuthan(1996). *A Textbook of Vāstuvidyā,* Vāstuvidyapratisthanam.
5. Ronald, M. Bernier (1982). *Temple Arts of Kerala.* S. Chand.
6. H. Sarkar. (1978). *An Architectural Survey of Temples of Kerala.* Archaeological survey of India.
7. Stella Kramrisch (1976).*The Hindu Temple.* Motilal Banarsidass.
8. K.V.Soundara Rajan (1974). *Temple Architecture in Kerala,* The Government of Kerala, Trivandrum.

9

THE MULTIFARIOUS MEANINGS OF A HOME IN THE CONTEXT OF KERALA

G. Reghukumar

Of all the riches of a land the most important is its cultural wealth. Culture is the quintessence of the achievements of a society in its totality attained through language, literature, education, architecture, politics, administration, etc. One of the significant aspects of any culture is its architecture. It is an art which rests on the foundation of a deep scientific awareness. The present paper aspires to discuss two important questions—which were the original concepts of style of the Keralites in the field of architecture? Has this influenced the architectural designs of contemporary times? And it offers certain directions and indications for the future developments in the field.

The paper comprises three sections. The first is a brief summing up of the Malayalee notions of a house. A discussion follows on the styles adopted by Kerala in the past in the field of artistic constructions and the mental, materialistic and ecological aspects related to it. An enquiry into how Kerala lost its artistic and ecological awareness in its architectural concerns follows. The paper is concluded with certain innovative directions on how art, science and ecology can be threaded to conceptualize the architectural concerns of the future.

As far as a Malayalee Keralite is concerned, a house is not just a place of residence. It is a space that calls you back again and again. Each individual is continuously addressed and called back in a voiceless language by his/her house. The ears of the soul are constantly tuned to listen to this language. This happens to be an innate truth. As in the case of the word 'mother' or '*mā*', a house also has multifarious meanings about it. From the moment of birth through the naturally sweet childhood and highly relished youth, an individual's identity and all basic awareness regarding notions of love and concern, friendship and cooperation is built on the foundation of the home from where the individual comes. Thus a home, which is the embodiment of all natural goodness is precious to each individual. Clear norms regarding the construction of a house—the where and how of it—were very much alive right from the distant past. *Mahāmanuṣyālayacandrikā* clearly details out the concepts of a house, a family and a village thus:

ekameva dvijāgarāṃ tatkuṭumbasamanvitam
ekabhogaṃ bhavetgrāmaṃ tat bhṛtyāyātanāvṛtam. (60)

That wholesome space can be called a village ('*grāmam*') where one resides with his wife, children and relatives, and with his servant community in those buildings suitable for each. This in turn can be reckoned a family. That space where one can reside with one's near and dear ones observing the right kind of rituals can be called a home. The *Manuṣyālayavidhī* refers to the land which is most suited for man's residence:

lakṣanamekakuṭumbasyālpam
parayunnathundu vidhīna njan
nalla niram saurabhyam
svadullatumuttamam nṛṇāṃ bhūmi. (9)

The land with the right kind of soil—dark, sweet smelling, and tasting good—is most suited for residence. The place meant for construction must be fragrant. The terrain and the tilt of the land were also paid much heed to. The most ideal place for the construction of a house is the land slightly tilted to the east facing the fields and with water flowing eastward in such a way that it can be checked with one's right hand. The *Manuṣyālayavidhī* specifies the traits to be sought after for a place of residence:

viprannuthara dikku thanathu subham, poorvanatham kshatriya nellarkkumsubhamakayundithu yameneecham thulom ninditham madhyam varunadikku thanathu pumanoohikka kanyanatham bhoomikkingane naluvarnanilayam veppanulam lakshanam. (11)

The land tilted to the north is especially good for Brahmins and the land tilted to the east is excellent for residence for all. As per the *Vāstuvallabha* astrological harmony essential for matrimonial matters is equally applicable for the construction of a house.

yaduktam gaṇayonyādi sarvaṃ dāmpatyakarmaṇi
tat sarvapi sañcintya bhuvi gehavidhau mitha

The *Manuṣyālayavidhī* dictates that the land has to be looked upon as a female and the house as the male and the horoscopic harmony to be analysed accordingly.

vedikā vanitā caiva grahaṃ tatra varo mataḥ
ubhayormitha sañcintyaṃ gaṇayonyādikaṃ śubham. (24)

Behind all actions rituals or '*pūjā*' and meditative ponderings were especially the norm in Kerala. This helped to reduce haughtiness and pride in man and to maintain faith and instil a healthy fear in the minds of all. The concept of *Vāstupuruṣa* emanates from the concepts on directions or '*dik*'.

pandekidappundoru dānavan kṣitau
per Vāstūpolasya kidappumingane
īṣāntakoṇe thala kalunairyate
jānukkal vayvahniyil hasta padayoho.
(*Bhāṣā Śilparatnam* 108)

The way *Vāstūpuruṣa* laid himself down to rest was taken seriously in the construction of houses in Kerala. Most works carry concepts and thoughts which could be marked ancient, superstitious and tainted with clear marks of Brahmin ascendancy despite the prevalence of certain truths in them.

All kinds of faith are superstitious and a blind obedience to any faith is illogical. Being sceptical of everything again is not a virtue. Faith must be manipulated as an inspiring force and thrust to all actions. In Keralite Vāstu concept there were many rules and concepts which were capable of inculcating wisdom in man.

Many ancient houses in Kerala are proud landmarks of the *vāstu* art tradition. In this art of construction in addition to intricate and embroidered artistic work certain rigid mathematical calculations were observed. Woodwork for roofing would be done on plain ground as the construction of the walls would proceed nearby. The calculation for wood work had to be perfect and exact for the different pieces of wood to dovetail atop the walls of the house to form the base for roofing. The senior carpenter who managed all the calculations without fail was called 'kanakkan', 'kanakku' being the term for mathematics in Malayalam. 'Uttaram', 'kazhukkol', 'vala', 'dwaram' all had to maintain the right proportion, the failure of which would lead to the 'uttaram' failing to get seated atop the wall. With great technical and mathematical expertise and with deep meditation and prayers the ancestors of the present Kerala community engaged themselves in the art of house construction. That again accounts for certain similarities perceived in the construction work of houses and other buildings of those times. A remarkable fact which is worth mentioning is that all these constructions were basically eco-friendly and environment-friendly leading to the well being of man and nature.

With the passage of time and intrusion of modernity drastic changes entered the thought processes and actions of modern man. The availability of cement and the nuclear family norms usurped the age-old practices and styles in house construction and all god-fearing sacred styles of functioning gave way to a materialistic mentality. Population hike, excess of illegal wealth, denial of tradition and erosion of values led to an absolute loss of mutuality. The stream of traditionally inherited knowledge slowly dried up without flowing into the minds of the new generation. The modern reckoned themselves wealthy with the knowledge of mechanical and IT skills. Value-based cultural notions of life have given way to this new knowledge, the hallmark of which is selfishness.

As in many other fields modernity affected changes even in the *vāstu* art. The divinity associated with a Malayalee house slowly eroded. This juncture in history demands discussions on the basis of our lost culture and the multifarious meanings of a house. Globalization and IT revolution have happened and the consequences of these have started gaining clarity. Modern times demand a merging of the achievements of new knowledge retaining well the virtues of our tradition.

The sense of unity and togetherness is lost. India was once a land of unified thinking. The unity emanated from the unifying strength of a tradition-based culture, denying all geographical variance and limitations. Today the light of unity has been put out by globalization. The sense of cultural mutuality which remained a strong binding force between men enabled them to discuss and rectify their mistakes. This has totally been erased and privatization has become the watchword in all fields of activity including the lives of men.

Competition started dominating all arenas of activity.

A person deprived of social relations and societal awareness is difficult to be brought under control. The people are least aware of what is called a healthy fear of society. Fellow beings are of least concern to modern man. Such people ought to be persuaded to behave favouring the land, culture and nation to which they belong for which they have to be brought under the control of governmental authority and observation.

Everything positive that is seen around is a creation of some meaningful cooperation. Art becomes practical through friendly relations. In a crowded desert deprived of the coolness of friendly relations, who can stand as the watch and ward of art, architecture and cultural values? A temporary system shall not suffice.

Modern man goes on constructing buildings with the money he has. Appropriate thought and discussion never enters into the making of it. When the small and pretty state of Kerala which was once the playground of prosperity and a proud culture is transformed unscrupulously into a cement forest without any artistic grace and elegance, firm and keen interference ought to be made.

The French thinker Michael Foucault had developed the notion of Panopticism. This was based on the design of the prison-house developed by the Englishman Jeremy Bentham. Public surveillance system which is rampant in controlling the traffic on streets and the monitoring of people who visit shops are all based consciously or unconsciously on the principle of panopticism. Rigid public surveillance is the only remedy to bring even the hostile construction of buildings in this land under check and control. Buildings constructed without any logical principles, thought and art must be caught by the eyes of a camera and people responsible for the violation of environmental, ecological, traditional and cultural values with reference to construction must be severely brought to task and compelled to effect corrections. All future constructions must be in accordance with the tradition, culture and environmental factors of a state. When such a norm is made rigid in all states the beauty and tradition of each region would be preserved without fail which would definitely be an invaluable suggestion for the present seminar to put forward.

To sum up all the matters discussed so far:

(1) In Kerala since time immemorial all actions were preceded with ritualistic prayers and offerings.
(2) Kerala had its original concepts on *vāstu* art, and faith in the lying posture of *vāstupuruṣa.*
(3) With the onset of modernity, by the 1960s, there arose a tendency to deny traditional values and to proclaim freedom in all areas of activity.
(4) Globalisation and the revolutionary advance of the modern Information Technology estranged the invaluable folk tradition and the natural flow of knowledge from folklore.
(5) Folklore was the essence of the unity of a community whereas modern knowledge is the essence of selfishness.
(6) All modern constructions set apart the identifying hallmarks of national, regional, environmental and traditional concepts on construction.
(7) Capturing the virtues of contemporary knowledge and linking it with the positive aspects of traditional *vāstu* art a new construction strategy has to be formulated. This is a crucial need of contemporary times.
(8) Governmental interference is most essential in this matter, and that too on a war footing. Strict surveillance and proper guidance to the public ought to be ensured.
(9) A construction art has to be formulated ensuring the fulfillment of a Keralite order enabling the

appropriate changes for the use of it by all sections of the society. Following the same path all the states can develop their own construction art and strategies thereby enabling a regional and cultural identity through the construction of homes and buildings.

The presenter of the paper hopes that the seminar would put forth certain suggestions towards the achievement of such a cultural identity in the field of construction of houses.

Bibliography

Bertens, Hans, *Literary Theory: The Basics*, London: Routledge, 2003.

Krishnan Jyolsyar, K. P. Comm. *Mahāmanuṣyālayacandrikā.* Kodungalloor: Devi Book Stall, 2008.

Neelakantanassari, *K. Jyolsyan. Manuṣyālayavidhī* Kodungalloor: Devi Book Stall, 2007.

Sreelekha, K.G. ed., *Bhashaśilparatnam,* Trivandrum Malayalam Series 178. Thiruvananthapuram: ORI & MSS Library, 2009.

10

VĀSTU CONCEPTS IN ARTHAŚĀSTRA

LALU S. KURUP

The Sanskrit word *vāstu* means a dwelling or house with a corresponding plot of land. *Śāstra* means science, doctrine, teaching, etc. In a broad sense, *vāstu* is an ancient Indian science of Architecture and building which helps in making a cogenial setting or a place to live and work in a most scientific way of taking advantage of the benefits bestowed by nature. *Vāstu* combines all the five elements of nature and balance them with the man and material. It also unifies the science, art, astrology and astronomy. This help, us to make our lives better and will secure from things going wrong.

The foundation of Vāstu is traditionally ascribed to the mythical Sage Mamuni Mayan. We can see the theories of Vāstuśāstra in the works of *Śilparatna, Thachuśāstram, Manuṣyālayacandirkā, Samarāṅgaṇasūtradhāra,* etc. From these works, we can retrive how to construct roads, houses, temples, palaces, etc.

Though the well known ancient Sanskrit work the *Arthaśāstra* is popularly considered to be an ideal text of state and politics, it sheds lights on the field of Vāstu also. In its present form, *Arthaśāstra* consists of 15 large sections called Adhikaraṇas, 150 adhyāyas, 180 sub-divisions styled Prakaraṇas and 6000 ślokas. In the second Adhikaraṇa of this work named *Adhyakṣapracāra*, Kauṭilya holds the relevance of Vāstu in constructing buildings in urban and rural areas. This paper aims to collect the Vāstu doctrines in Kauṭilya's *Arthaśāstra.*

Structure of Villages

In the Mauryan period, the local unit of administration is called Janapada. In the *Arthaśāstra* the first chapter that is, Janapadanivesa begins with an advice to the ruler, how to set up a good Janapada. According to Kauṭilya, the Janapada belongs to the people brought either from the excess populated area of the kingdom or from adjoining areas. The range of families in each Janapada were varied from 100 to 500. The majority of population in Janapada were the Śūdras engaged in cultivation.

The Janapada unit had a size of one to two *krosa.* The geographical indication including rivers, mountains, hills, trees were bases for demarcating the boundaries of a Janapada from one to other. In the 19th Prakaraṇa of *Arthaśāstra,* Kauṭilya tells about the boundaries of villages. The well-planed entry gates were built in the four directions of each village. The self-sufficiency and progress of the Emperor largely depends on the cultivation and other agriculture based activities of each Janapada. Therefore Kauṭilya gave importance to the routines of people in the Janapada.

Township Construction

According to the *Arthaśāstra,* township had a vast size of 1000 *daṇḍa* to 2000 *daṇḍu* cm.[2] The township carries state capital which constituted the middle of 800 Janapadas. The township was adjoined with Droṇamukha, Kharvadika and Sangrahaṇa.

Forts

Forts are the manmade obstacles to defend external

invation. According to the *Arthaśāstra,* there are four types of forts (*durgas*). They are *audaka, pārvata,* Dhanvāna and Vana.

Durgas

It is the prime duty of the king to built store rooms for the storage of grains for future use. The *Vāstu* principles are to be considered while finding place for grainhouse. These houses were either square or cirle and near the river. The forts protected the grainhouse and Kauṭilya's *Arthaśāstra* reveals more about the construction of forts.

Walls

The forts are encircled with long walls. Soil and rocks are mainly used for constructing these walls. Poison creapers are planted on the sides of walls. For chariot transportation, roads were constructed on the top of the walls. Kauṭilya prohibited the use of wood for the construction of walls.

Royal Passages

The details of royal passages were narrated in the 22nd Prakaraṇa of the *Arthaśāstra.* According to Kauṭilya an ideal state must have six main passages. Among the six passages, three were constructed to connect the east-west province and the other three were connected the north-south parts of the state.

Rājaniveśa

By considering the roots of *vāstu,* Kauṭilya recommended that, the royal palace (*rājaniveśa*) was located on the northern part of the capital city. The north and east sides of the *Rajaniveśa* were used for building the residence of the *purohitha* and ācārya. The south and east sides of the *Rajanivesa* were used to build rest houses for elephants. The Kṣatriyas can use the east side of the Rājaniveśa for constructing their residence. The Vaiśya houses were located in the southern part of the state.

Crematorium

Kauṭilya prescribes building separate crematoriums for different castes. The crematorium for the upper caste people were built on the north-east side of the Rājaniveśa. But the crematorium of Śūdra communiy were situated on the northern part of the Janapada.

Conclusion

From the above narration, it is very clear that, the Mauryas showed special interest in the field of Vāstu. They gave due importance to the environment and yielded special attention to the construction of their buildings to make them eco friendly.

References

1. Ayappa Panicker K, (Gen: Editor), *Kawtalyan ArthaŚāstram,* Kottayam: D.C., Books, 2010.
2. Manoj, S. Nair, *Vāstuvidya Kshethravidhanam,* Kottayam: Dept. of Printing and Publishing, M.G. University and Vāstu Vidya Gurukulam, 2008.
3. Niranjan Babu B., *Vāstu: Relevence to Modern times,* Kottayam D.C.Books, 2006.
4. Raghavanachari Kidangoor, *Śilpavidyā Prakāśikā,* Kottayam, D.C Books, 2007.
5. Rangarajan L.N, Kautilya The ArthaŚāstra, New Delhi: Penguin Books, 1992.
6. Samba Śiva Sastri K. (Editor), Kautiliyam-II *Bhasha Vyakhyana Sahitam,* Thiruvananthapuram: Dept. of Publications, University of Kerala, 1972.
7. Vamanan Namboothiri, *Vāstumana Prāmanangal,* Kottayam: D.C. Books, 2007.

11

TEMPLE ARCHITECTURE IN ĪŚĀNAŚIVAGURUDEVAPADDHATI AND NATIVITY OF ĪŚĀNAŚIVAGURU

K.S. Bindusree

Kerala's contribution to Tantra literature in Sanskrit is great. Kerala is a land of temples too. Tantra texts deal with temple architecture. The *Prapañcasāra* of Śrī Śaṅkara, the *Prayogamañjarī* of Ravi Nambutiri, the *Īśānaśivagurudevapaddhati* (ISGP) of *Īśānaśivaguru* and the *Tantrasamuccaya* of Chennas Narayanan Namputiri are notable contributions of Kerala in this field. ISGP follows the Śaiva Āgamas. ISGP is also called *Tantrasāra, Tantrapaddhati, Siddhāntasāra,* etc.

Identity and nativity of Īśānasivaguru are matters of conjecture. The present paper is an attempt to make a brief analysis of the temple architecture dealt with in the ISGP and to relate the same to Kerala temples with a view to determining the author's native place.

Date

The ISGP follows the Śaivāgama-tradition. The *Jayākhyasaṃhitā* is the earliest scripture which makes mention of *Bhūtaśuddhi* or purification of the elements in connection with the use of pots for *abhiśeka* or consecration of temples. The pocedure of *bhūtaśuddhi* mentioned in *Jayākhya* is accepted by Somaśambhu in his Tantra text Somaśambhupaddhati which is followed by the Śaivas along with the ISGP. Somaśambhu was an abbot of the monastery of Golaka in Tamil Nadu. His date is second half of the eleventh century. Somaśambhu is mentioned and followed in many respects by *Īśānaśivaguru.* So *Īśānaśivaguru* can be safely located after eleventh century AD. It is believed by many scholars including Dr.N.P. Unni that he lived in the twelfth century AD.[1]

ISGP

The ISGP was found out from Kerala, but it does not assure the author's nativity of Kerala. Dr.T.Ganapati Sastri adds the suffix Miśra to the name Īśānaśivagurudeva.[2] Miśra is taken to be a non-Keralite name and the nativity of the author is decided accordingly. Dr. T. Ganapati Sastri supports the argument that the author of ISGP was a native of Kosala or Mithila.

The ISGP is divided into four pādas, namely Samanvayapāda, Mantrapāda, Kriyāpāda and Yogapāda. Samanvayapāda has 14 paṭalas, Mantrapāda 38 paṭalas, Kriyāpāda 64 paṭalas and Yogapāda 3 paṭalas. Totally there are 119 paṭalas. Altogether it has 18,000 stanzas.

The general principles regarding the Tantric rites and rituals to be performed as part of building construction are dealt with in the Samanvayapāda of ISGP. The second quarter of the ISGP, as the name Mantrapāda indicates, is dedicated to deal with the mantras to be chanted on various occasions. The third quarter, as indicated by the name Yogapāda, deals with Yoga especially the Yoga of Patañjali. The fourth quarter which is the largest of the ISGP is completely devoted to deal with matters regarding construction.

The ISGP can be considered to be a mini encyclopedia. Protection of house, subjugation by enchantment, jugglery, Yoga, different kinds of treatments, *Japa, Homa,* the science of magic and the construction of buildings have been the topics. Temple architecture is a major subject in the ISGP. Selection of the site, laying of the foundation, structure of the temple, construction of the temple, sculpture of idols and their types, installation of idols, consecration and the rituals related to all these have been dealt with in the ISGP.

Selection of site

The most important step in the construction of a temple is the selection of land. Land should be located in a very sacred place. The ISGP has made some important observations in the selection of land. The place should be surrounded by rivers and mountains and the land should be fertile. The land is divided into two types: *sāmānya* and *saṅkīrṇa.* The land, whch is favoured by Vedic poets and Brahmins, where trees are densely grown, which is the source of good wealth, which faces waterfalls, which is surrounded by plants bearing fruits and flowers, where cows pasture freely and which has plenty of water are enlisted under *sāmānya.* Saṅkīrṇa type of land is not usually chosen by the people belonging to the four varṇas.

Rituals

Some important rituals are to be conducted as part of the temple construction. The patron who intends to construct a temple should approach a high priest who is to be worshipped by eight other priests at the behest of the patron. The eight priests are supposed to be the eight forms of Śiva. The patron should worship the high priest and request him to take charge of the ceremony along with others. The next ritual is warding off evil spirits. This is conducted by the high priest before the beginning of the plunging in a ceremony. The land is to be tilled by others and seeds are to be sown by uttering the names of Vāmadeva.

Temple precinct

The site is sprinkled with water and cowdung mixed together. The boundary is demarcated with an iron hammer and stumps are fixed. The area is then cleared of all its vegetation.

Vāstudevatā

Vāstudevatā is to be worshipped by performing *vāstupūjā* in the proposed site. There are a number of stories connected with the *Vāstudevatā* in the Indian mythology related to architecture. The ISGP also deals with such stories. The *Vāstupuruṣa* is supposed to be lying on the site stretching his legs to the north-east and placing his head towards the south-west. The ISGP quotes the story of *Vāstupuruṣa* from Somaśambhu to show the importance of *vāstupūjā*.

Laying the foundation

The first brick is to be placed in a pit which is to be dug to the depth of the height of a man with his hands raised. The bricks should be properly baked and should be unbroken. Each corner of the plot joins seven other columns by drawing lines. A number of points where the lines cross one another will emerge and these are called *marmas*. Pits are to be dug at *marmas*.

Temple structure

The design of temples that prevailed between the twelfth and fourteenth centuries has been dealt with in the ISGP. It presents a detailed account of the special features that flourished in the design and structures of temples.

It is not within the scope of the present paper to go into all the details of temple architecture dealt with in the ISGP. The concern here is to assess the application of the details of temple architecture dealt within the ISGP in the construction of Kerala temples.

The temple architecture tradition of Kerala comes within that of the mainstream of Indian tradition. In the detailed articulation of its formal structure Kerala temple follows its own indigenous methods, but the basic conceptions are not different from the total architectural developments of India.

Early sources like the *Bṛhatsaṃhitā* classify temples based on norms of proportionate measure and they list twenty possible shapes of *prāsāda.* The texts on architecture, classify temples into three different styles: the Nāgara or 'northern' style, the Drāviḍa or 'southern ' style and the Vesara or hybrid style which is seen in the Deccan between the other two. The ISGP follows the *prāsāda-vimāna* classification of structures in general and the Nāgara-Drāviḍa-Vesara classification of vimāna.[3] There are also distinct styles in peripheral areas such as Bengal, Kerala and the Himalayan valleys. But by far the most numerous buildings are in either the Nāgara or the Drāviḍa styles and the earliest surviving structural temples can be seen as falling into the broad classifications of either one or the other.

Construction of the structural temples which began in the eighth century AD was patronized by Chera, Āy and Mushaka kings. The ruler and the leading chiefs and landholders vied with one another in liberal endowments for the construction and maintenance of the temples. Apart from this, the inflow of wealth into the country arising from Kerala's prosperous overseas trade had brought into existence, an affluent mercantile community during this period. A vast majority of the ancient temples that we find in Kerala today had their origin during this period. Various types of temple structure, like square, circular and apsidal originated during this period. The presence of *Sapta Mātṛkā* images datable to this period also proves the prevalence of rectangular shrines. Square *vimāṇas* antidate the other ones because all the cave temples conform to this type.

Temples in Kerala used to be called *ambala* or *kṣetra* or sometimes *tali.* The Kerala temple has *Śrikovil* as its main core, which usually stands in east-west axis and the plan may be square, rectangular, circular, elliptical or apsidal ground plan. Compared to the other temple styles in the mainland like Drāviḍa, Nāgara and Vesara, Kerala temple tradition has distinct characteristics especially in their formal structure. The architectural style of Kerala temples has an inherent simplicity which becomes very conspicuous when juxtaposed to the exuberance of the Nāgara, Vesara and Drāviḍa temple styles. In explaining this, influence of the natural environment upon the temple form has to be recognized along with the socio-historical developments.

The basic relationship of the particular landscape which contains and holds the respective architectural form is a major deciding factor. Between the two, an organic unity and balance exist, which keep on interacting with each other. The environmental space which envelopes the architecture has a major role in the articulation of architectural form. This interdependence or the reciprocal relationship between environment and architecture can be further noticed in the construction of superstructures in Kerala temples. The two monsoons a year, and the humidity in Kerala weather has a direct bearing on the use of sloping roofs and the selection of raw materials by which the superstructure is being constructed.

The superstructure as a conspicuous example shows an accurate usage of indigenous raw materials like timber and tiles to go with the climatic conditions. Vast majority of temples have their bases built of granite, the walls made either of wood, bricks and stucco, or laterite; the sloping superstructure made of wooden planks, tiles or sheet metal on timber frames, are adopted to suit the high rainfall of the region. The roof timbers rest directly on the wall and coverage in gable form to meet at the top. The roofing material covering the timber framework is clinker built. It is made up of wooden planks overlapping one another, and covered over by clinker tiles or tiles highly heated in kilns with a glazy smooth surface that makes them waterproof. The details given above substantiate that the raw materials used are meant to withstand the damp weather.

A truly indigenous contribution to the mainstream of Indian architectural tradition is the circular temples. The ponderous appeal of the sloping conical superstructure above the circular basement and walls is a clear testimony of the local idiom. Further, the edge of the superstructure comes down to join in hugging the earth. The height of the superstructure is further softened by the circular mould bands which function to accent down the verticality and emphasize the horizontality. The symmetry of the circle does not hamper fine nuances and modulations of the wall below. The spread of the conical roof above the wide cylinder, formed by the circular wall gives to the structure at the same time, a buoyant lift and a light winged aeriality. As a matter of fact, conical roof is the most satisfactory logical solution for the enclosure built on a circular plan. In a few cases, the rhythm of the circular temples is further extended into elliptical shape.

Most of the temples, some with original *adiṣṭhāna,* dating from eighth-ninth centuries have considerably renovated superstructures. So they do not reveal much of their original forms. The difficulty in exactly verifying the principles and specifications laid down by the ISGP in the structures of Kerala temples is mainly this. The author of the ISGP might have taken into account the structures of the Kerala temples of those days in writing the book. He has also incorporated in his work the teachings of a long line of Saiddhāntikas who were influential all over India during the ninth-eleventh centuries and later.[4]

The major parts of a typical Kerala temple

The parts of Kerala temples are calculated based on many schemes. According to one scheme the major parts are twenty in number. They are as follows:

1.*Devapratiṣṭhā or Idol*

Devapratiṣṭhtā or idol of God or Goddess is the most important part of a Hindu temple. Idols made of granite, *pañcaloha,* or wood is usually installed inside the *Garbhagṛha* or Śrīkovil. Idols are made according to the *dhyānaślokas.* Apart from the normal daily worship, rituals for propitiating the deities, there are many Tantric rituals aiming at increasing the glory and power of the deities and sometimes for atonement for any fading of such power.

2. Śrīkovil or Sanctum Sanctorum

The part of the temple where the idol of God or Goddess is situated is referred to as the *Śrīkovil*. The position of *Śrikovil* in the temple is equivalent to the position of Sahasrāra padma in a human body.

The *Śrīkovil* may be in square, rectangular, elliptical or circular shape and may have one two or even three stories covered with copper or gold. A *Śrīkovil* or *garbhagṛha* having two walls and a corridor in between these walls is of *śāntara* style. If the *Śrīkovil* has only one wall it is of *nīrantara* style. The top of the sanctum has a pointed bronze or gold structure called Tazhikakkudam or *stūpikā*.

3. *Sopāna*

The holy steps in front of the sanctum sanctorum are called *sopāna*. In many temples the *sopāna* has stone idols of guards of God called *dvārapālakas*. Usually *sopāna* is covered with gold or bronze. Sabarimala Temple has gold covered sopāna and *dvārapālakas*. Only temple priests are allowed to enter through these holy steps.

4. *Pradakṣiṇavatta or Akathe balivattam*

It is located just outside the sanctum. The *Aṣṭa-Dik-pālakas* (Indra, Agni, Yama, Nirṛti, Varuṇa, Vāyu, Soma and Īśāna), Sapta Mātṛkās (Brahmāṇi, Māheśvarī, Kaumāri, Vaiṣṇavī, Varāhī, Indrāṇī and Cāmuṇḍī), Vīrabhadra, Gaṇapati, Śāstā, Ananta, Durgā, Subrahmaṇya, Kubera, Nirmālyadhārī and Brahmā. The guards of the main deity are represented here by stones of different shapes and are generally called Balikkallu. Usually these balikkallus are covered with bronze sheets. Pradakṣiṇavatta of Kazhakuttom Mahādeva Temple and Balikkallu representing Yama of Anandavalliśvaram

Temple, Kollam are good examples.

5. *Mātṛśālā*

Mātṛśālā is located in the south side of *Śrīkovil.* It is an extended portion of Nalambalam towards *Śrīkovil* to cover the *Saptamātṛbalikkallu.* Hence the name *Mātṛśālā.* Usually the *Utsavabali* ritual is performed in the *Mātṛśālā.*

6. *Namaskāra-maṇḍapa*

Namaskāra-maṇḍapa is located in front of the *sopāna* facing the sanctum. It is used by the priests for *Sāṣṭāṅga namaskāra* after *pūjās* like Usha *pūjā,* Panthiradi *pūjā* and Uccha *pūjā.* Hence is the name *Namāskāra-maṇḍapa.* It is generally square in shape and has a roof hung by four pillars and usually has a Tazhikakkudam made of gold or copper. Usually *Vedajapa* and *Kalasapūjā* are done at the *Namaskāra*-maṇḍapa and so it is also called *Kalasa-maṇḍapa.* In Śiva temples it is called Nandi-maṇḍapa because of the presence of Nandi and in Viṣṇu temples it is called *Garuḍa-maṇḍapa* because of the presence of Garuḍa.

7. *Nalambalam and Valiambalam*

Nalambalam is also called Chuttambalam. Their function is to protect the temple as they cover the temple on all sides. They are less broad on the surrounding three sides and are called Chuttambalam. The one facing the sanctum is very broad and is called Valiambalam. Between the two Valiambalams there is a passage for devotees to enter and exit.

8. *Thidappally*

Thidappally is the kitchen of a temple. Thidappally is constructed on the left side of the *Namaskāra-maṇḍapa* as an enclosure in the south eastern corner of the Nalambalam. *Naivedyams* to be offered to the deity are prepared in the Thidappally. None other than the priests and *Tantrī* of the temple is allowed inside the Thidappally.

9. *Mulayara*

Mulayara is a special room of the Chuttambalam and is used for Mūlapūjā on special days like *Utsavam, Sahasra-Kalasam* and *Aṣṭabandha Kalasam.*

10. *Well*

A well is a must in a temple. Its position is at the north-east, of the Nalambalam. Its water has to be exclusively used for *abhiṣeka* or preparation of *naivedya.*

11. *Vilakkumadam*

Another distinctive feature of Kerala temples is the use of Vilakkumadam, or the multi-tiered brass lamps in front of temples. Lakṣadīpa is a spectacular celebration of traditional lighting where tiers of small oil lamps lining the outer walls of the inner *prākāra* are lit. It is located outside the Nalambalam. In between the Nalambalam and Vilakkumadam there may be an open area. Only Mahā-kṣetras will have seperate Vilakkumadam. In small temples multi-tiered brass lamps are fixed on the Nalambalam itself.

12. *Balikkalpura*

It faces the sanctum and is the extended portion of the passage in between the Valiyambalams. The large, Valiya Balikkallu (principal bali-pīṭha) is located here. Size of the Valiya Balikkallu depends on the size and height of the Śrīkovil. The roof of the Balikkalpura may have the wooden sculptures of Aṣṭadikpalākas and Devī. Valiyabalikkallu is also decorated with sculptures. But in temples like Kudal-manikyam there is no Balikkalpura for Valiya Balikkallu.

13. *Dhvaja or Kodimaram*

This tall pillar is visible from a distance. It bears on the top the deity's *vāhana* as emblem and one can identify the deity of a temple by seeing it. Śiva temple has Nandi, Viṣṇu temple has Garuḍa, Durgā temple has Lion, Kālī temple has Vetāla, Śāstā temple has Horse, Subrahmaṇya temple has Peacock, Gaṇapati temple has Mūṣika and Sarasvatī temple has Haṃsa on top of the dhvaja. Aṣṭadikpālaka idols are placed at the bottom of the dhvaja. Kodimaram is used for hoisting kodi or flag during festivals. It is located outside the Balikkalpura and is usually made of wood and covered with copper, *pañcaloha,* silver, bronze or gold.

14. *Anakkottil*

Anakottil facing Balikkalpura is located in front of the dhvaja . It is the place where elephants stand during festivals. It is also used for functions like marriage, chorunu, parayeduppu, thulabharam and bhajans.

15. *Shivelippura and Pradakṣiṇa Vazhi:*

Shivelippura or Shribalippura is not so common in Kerala temples. This is the place used for *Kazhcha Śrībali.* Padmanābha Swami Temple of Thiruvananthapuram and Guruvayoor Temple have beautiful Shivelippuras. In other temples instead of Shivelippura there will be a *Pradakṣiṇa* Vazhi in the Thirumuttam.

16. *Uttupura*

Uttupura is the dining hall of a temple. In the past only Brahmins were allowed to take food from Uttupura. Nowadays, they are used for *Annadānam* and *Varāsādya* meant for all. It will have a large kitchen. In some temples like Vaikom and Ambalappuzha the Uttupura is as sacred as the temple *Śrīkovil.*

17. *Kutthambalam*

The Kutthambalam or the theatre hall of the Kerala temple is located on the south-east corner of Nalambalam. This is the place where the performance of Chakyarkuthu and Kudiyattam art forms, are held. Kutthambalams are usually in rectangular shape and has three parts. *Raṅgapīṭha* or stage raised from the rest of the floor, Nepathyam or green room and a Prekṣakagṛham for viewers. Kutthambalams are often decorated with large number of wood sculptures. Thus the Kutthambalam plays a role in educating visitors on the rich legends of the Indian cultural fabric. Kutthambalams in temples like Thriśivaperoor, Thirunakkara, Thiruvarppu, Harippad, Kidangoor, Arpookkara and Irinjalakkuda are famous for their sculptures. In some temples like Trippunithura Śrī Purnathrayisa temple, Kutthambalam is a part of Nalambalam.

18. *Gopūram*

Major temples will have four *Gopūrams in* east, west, south and north. Śri Padmanabha Svami Temple of Thiruvananthapuram is the only temple in Kerala having a huge *Gopūram* with stone works. The four *Gopūrams* of Aranmula Parthasarathy Temple and Thrissur Śrī Vadakkumnatha Temple are examples of typical Kerala style. The four *Gopūrams* are connected to the outer compound wall of the temple. There is the typical Kerala style of architecture of temple towers and it varies from single to multistoried.

19. *Mathil or Outer walls*

These are the outermost protective coverings of the temple. Major temples are well protected with huge compound walls.

20. *Thirthakkulam*

Nearly every temple has a sacred pond or Thirthakkulam and kulappura outside the temple wall if there is no river nearby. Normally, the temple pond is located on the north-east corner of the temple. The water of the temple pond is used for washing one's hands and feet before going into the temple, bathing and sometimes for the Arattu ceremonies.

A temple having all these elements is called a *Mahākṣetra* (great temple) or Perumthrkkovil. There are a number of Mahākṣetras in Kerala.

Pañca-prākāra scheme

The details given above are sometimes reduced to a *Pañca-Prākāra* scheme. As the term indicates, the five enclosures around the sanctum are as follows:

1. Akatthe-Balivattam—The innermost enclosure, which includes the *Śrīkovil, Antar-mandala,* Bali-Kallu and *Namaskāra-maṇḍapa.*
2. Nalambalam/Chuttambalam—Around the sanctum consists of Valiambalam, Thitappalli and Mulayara.
3. Madhyahara/Vilakkumatam—The 'Galaxy of Lamps'.
4. Puratthe-Balivattam/Sivelippura, Outer cnclosure and cirumabulatory pathway consisting of Agra-maṇḍapa, Valiya-balikkallu, Bali-pīṭha, Kṣetra-pāla, Dhvaja-stambha, Kovil of minor deities and Kuthambalam.
5. Maryādā/Puram Mathil—The outer boundary wall with Gopura, Uttu-pura and Puram-mathil.

The Kerala temple walls are made of coursed laterite stone masonry plastered in mud and lime. Murals are seen on several of these temple walls.

The Kerala temple is an amalgam of stonework, wood work, stucco work and painting, harmoniously blended into a structure. The wood work here is of great importance, and it gives the essential character to the Kerala temple. The inner skeletal framework of the temple is of wood, and the base and the structure above are of granite and laterite respectively. The roof projects out at several levels, in order to protect the inner skeletal framework. This is in view of the protection from the vigorous monsoons prevalent in the region.

The Drāviḍa type of temple construction described in the ISGP fits in Kerala temples. Of course there have been several improvements made by the architects. Actually theory and practice are inseparable. Theory is improved by practice. This applies to temple architecture also.

There is an argument that the temple culture of Kerala is based on Vedic moorings, in contrast to the Agamic traditions of Tamil Nadu. It is a fact that Kerala temples of the present day exhibits presence of Vedic influence. But this would not have been the case ever since the origin of temple culture. In fact the Vedic and temple traditions are entirely different. The former is that of sacrifices whereas the latter has nothing to do with sacrifices. It was only much later that the Vedic Brahmins crept into the temple tradition.

The ISGP represents a period when Brahmanism had already occupied key positions in the temple tradition. It may be noted in this connection that the ISGP deals with the details of temple construction in strict accordance with Cāturvarṇya.

The structure of Kerala temples represents *vimānas* and *prāsādas*. *Vimānas* imply different specifications with regard to each and every measurement of the building. *Prāsāda* mainly implies the pleasure obtained by residing in the building. *Prāsādas* generally denote Nāgara type and *Vimānas* Drāviḍa type of temples. *Vimānas* are of two kinds namely Jātivimānas and Jātitaravimānas. Jātīvimānas are meant for the Brahmins, Kṣatriyas, Vaiśyas and Śūdras. Twelve types of Vimānas are designed for Brahmins, twenty-four for Kṣatriyas, eight for Vaiśyas and eight again for Śūdras. The ISGP deals with all these details. Thus a total of fifty-two structures have been enumerated in the ISGP.

The ISGP mentions about *Mukhya* type of *Vimānas* also.

All the three kinds namely *Jāti, Jātītara* and *Mukhya* are designed in the same pattern as that of Nāgara, Drāviḍa and Vesara. The structures which come under the category of *Mukhya* are designed as the abodes of the trinity namely Brahmā, Viṣṇu and Śiva.

Descriptions of, different parts of temple from the basement to the sanctum sanctorum, pedestal of idol, pillars, *Prastāra, Dvāra, Gopūra, Śikhara,* Storeys, *Sopānas,* structures like Nalinakam, Svasthikam, Chaturmukham, sanctum sanctorum, drains, *maṇḍapas,* walls, rites and rituals etc. available in the ISGP concur with the structure of Kerala temples. Based on this, it can be ascertained that Īśānaśivaguru was a native of Kerala.

References

1 *Īśānaśivagurudevapaddhati,* 4 vols. ed. Dr. N.P. Unni, Delhi, 1987.
2. *Īśānaśivagurudevapaddhati,* vol. I, ed. T. Ganapati Sastri, Trivandrum, 1920, p. 71.
3. *Īśānaśivagurudevapaddhati,* 3, 28, 3–4.
4. Stella Kramrisch, *The Hindu Temple,* vol. I, Delhi, 1976, p. 286.

12

DRAVIDIAN TEMPLE ARCHITECTURE: ŚRĪ PADMANĀBHA SWAMY TEMPLE- A CASE STUDY

VYSAKH. A.S.

The fame and glory of the ancient city of Thiruvananthapuram, the capital of the state of Kerala attributes to the majestic Śrī Padmanābha Swamy Temple centuries before and even to the present. Encompassed by numerous tales and legends, the antiquity of its origin is still shrouded in mystery. The Padmanābha Swamy reigns as the tutelary deity of the Travancore royal family and forms the heart beat of the people of Thiruvananthapuram.Two distinct aspects were associated with this temple. From the time it is known, it enjoyed the stature of a *Mahakṣetram*(Great temple) and it was all along interconnected with royalty. The temple is identified as one among the 108 *Tirupatties* or great temples of Viṣṇu, one among the seven *Muktisthalas* or spiritual seats of salvation and as one among the six *Nārāyaṇasthalas* or centres of Vaishnavite divinity in India. The earliest known records of this temple appear in the Epics and Purāṇas and the first reference to its sanctity is seen in the *Syanandoora-Purāṇa-Samuchayam* of AD 1168, followed by literary and epigraphical sources.

The concept of 'Śrī Padmanābha' is one among the twenty-four visualizations of Śrī Mahāviṣṇu. Here the great *Perumal* (lord) is worshipped as the ever blissful one who is the very embodiment of peace as also the one reclining on the mighty

Ananta (serpent) in conscious slumber. Since the *Padma* or Lotus spirals up from his *nābhi* or navel, he bears the name 'Padmanābha'.

The temple owes its present magnanimity to the devotion of numerous ruling families that had ruled the *Malayala* Nadu (Kerala) in the bygone era. Despite the changes in the names of the ruling houses,the Padmanābha Swamy Temple had received continued emotional allegiance and royal patronage. To quote Gouri Lekshmi Bayi in Śrī Padmanābha Swamy Temple, "As the dynastic deity as well as personal deity of the royal lines who held sovereignty over this land, the temple and the throne were interlinked by bonds which stood the test of time.The Temple coloured all activities of the State and their interests overlapped and became one."

The deity became the temporal as well as the spiritual Head, the monarch of the State of Travancore with the famed '*Trippadi Daanam*' the deed and dedication of the whole territory by the Maharaja Anizham Tirunal Marthanda Varma, the founder of modern Travancore on January 20, 1750. All honours thus reserved for the sovereign were transferred to Śrī Padmanābha Swamy and the kings of Travancore thenceforth ruled only as the servants of the Lord. Surprisingly even the British Government recognized the deity as the real ruler. And it is therefore unique in the world history of religion that a deity be recognized as the constitutional head of the state and government even by the foreign powers whose overlordship existed at that time. History stands as an exception here, that no invader had ever dared to gaze at this abode of the Lord of wealth and remained free from any ravages of plundering wars or external invasions, thus adding to its supreme power and treasure since its inception. Apart from its unending historical connections and royal patronages, the temple is a treasure house of art and architecture as well. Too much space will be required if a detailed description of its architectural and artistic treasures is embarked upon, consequently only a brief introduction to this structural extravaganza is envisaged here. The temple received its present form after the major renovation carried out under Marthanda Varma.

Architecturally the Dravidian style is predominant as such,but the overall structural pattern locates an intermingling of Kerala-Tamil(Dravidian) styles of vāstu and patterns are evident. Though this is the case, the Nayik influence with distinct local flavour could also be traced. To the whole, Śrī Padmanābha Swamy Temple is an amalgamation of the Dravidian, Chola, Pandya and the Kerala styles of architecture which complement and not contradict each other.The treatises used for the construction of the temple include the *Śilparatna, Syanandoora-purāṇa-Samuchayam, Īśānśivagurudevapaddhati,* etc. along with incorporations from Dravidian and other indigenous texts. As this remains the fact, this article concentrates on the Dravidian aspects of the temple along with the various amalgamations.

It is the Rajagopūram (tower) abounding with figures and decorations that characterises the Padmanābha Swamy Temple. The Tamil style was a deliberate incorporation, and was unavoidable as the southern regions of Tamil Nadu were often under the rule of Travancore.The close cultural affinity was thus recognized and cemented it with the emotional fusion of the two major linguistic groups,—the Malayalees and the Tamils.

The present form and structures we see today in the Padmanābha Swamy Temple took shape during the reign of Anizham Tirunal Marthanda Varma(1729-58), the architect of modern Travancore, who renovated the temple.The king took pains to keep the ancient character and the originality of the same, thereby preserving it as an everlasting monument of his undettered devotion to the deity. Earlier in AD 1686, during the reign of King Iravi Varma, a great fire engulfed most of the temple complex which was originally made of wood. And hence during its renovation a great deed of conservation was shown by Marthanda Varma by deciding the extensive use of granite.The responsibility of the work was entrusted to Viṣṇu Thratan Namboodiri of Thycaud Illom and Anantha Padmanābhan Asari being the chief mason, while the Maharaja took upon himself the task of supervision at every stage.

Hereafter, it would be pleasing to enter into the architectural wonder of the temple covering upon a circumambulation in the vast canvas of vision.

Poetry in Stone–Architecture and Structure

The Padmanābha Swamy Temple rests at a moderate elevation on about seven acres of land enclosed within high granite walls on its four sides overlooking the Agasthya mountains on the east. The granite boundary walls contain isolated engravings here and there including the ones of Mārkaṇḍeya, Śāsta, floral and animal design, etc., thereby turning itself into a huge canvas. On either side of the path leading to the temple, is seen the famed sacred pond 'Padmatīrtham' on the right and a row of the palatial buildings uniquely in Kerala style on the left.

A flight of thirteen steps (it is believed that originally they were eighteen and five of them got buried in the sand) lead to the main entrance of the temple. The steps lead to the portico, the roof of which being supported by two elegantly carved mighty figure of *Vyali* (dragon)on either side depicting an essential feature of Kerala architecture. One enters into the lofty and spacious hall called the 'Natakasala Mukhappu'. It is the area embarked for conducting drama, dance, musical recitals, scholarly discourses, etc., the holding of such temple arts being an exquisite feature in Kerala temples. The hall being 120 feet long and 48 feet wide with two raised platforms on either side for the spectators. A specially constructed carved wooden room on the left raised platform is reserved for the royal ladies to watch the performances. Moderately carved four rows of ten fluted pillars in the hall supports the roof.

The self imposing, 'Gopūram' has its own uniqueness, standing separate from any other temple in Kerala. The structure, dimension and symbolism that it emanates is unparalled. As delineated earlier the 'Gopūram' was constructed as an unifying aspect of the two related cultures—the Tamil and Malayalee. Hence this very structure could be seen only in the two temples under the erstwhile Travancore, they being the Suchindram Temple in Tamil Nadu and one at the Padmanābha Swamy Temple. The foundation stone for the imposing *Gopūram* was laid in the time of King Aditya Varma in AD 1565 and goes about forty feet deep. The first five stories of the present *Gopūram* was constructed at the time of Mārtanda Varmā during its major renovation in 1929 and the last two by Maharaja Karthika Tirunal Rāma Varma. The *Gopūrām* is made up of brick, lime and mortar on granite base rising to about one hundred feet with steps leading right upto the floor. Seven globe like structures called the 'Thazhikakkudams' are placed on the boat shaped ornamentation right on the top of the *Gopūrām*. The boat shaped structure peculiar with its structure, stands unique and is an uncommon feature in *Gopūrāms*. This ornamentation is symbolical, depicting Vanchi Nadu which is another appellation for this state, the *Vanchi* or boat itself being displayed. The association with *Kola Swaroopam* and another indicative of prosperity are implied with this typical structure. Each floor carries a window—like opening (niche) in the centre guarded by two *Dvārapālakas*. The *Gopūram* itself is incorporated with more than two hundred odd figures and figurines each different from the other. The first floor contains numerous carvings of deities including the depiction of *Ananta-śayanam*. A panoramic and enchanting view of the city spreads like a feast before the eyes from the top floor of the *Gopūram*, also visible is the distant view of the Agastya ranges in the east and the lined depiction of the Arabian sea in the west.

On ascending the *Gopūram,* protruding columns have been worked out in the central area indicative of the later Chola style constructions.The base of the same displays themes from Hindu Purāṇas including the Mahābhārata and Rāmāyaṇa presented with a wealth of expert craftsmanship and creativity.Two huge *Dvārapālakas* depicted in great detail are seen on the platform on either side of the floor level of *Gopūram.* A pair of single stone, one vertical and the other horizontal make up the main door frame, with four elephant heads with raised trunks pretend to support the weight of the *Gopūram* on their backs.The entrance corridor too has depictions of artistic reliefs and exclusively depicted works from the Purāṇas.

A small corridor connects the *Seevelippura* (path for circumambulation) with six pillars. On these pillars are carved the figure of the chief *sthapati* or mason Anantha Padmanābhan Moothasari and his family as well as the replicas of the tools used, right in front of the *Dhvajastambha* (flagstaff) and entrance to the sanctum sanctorum. The *Seevelippura* being one of the masterpieces in this temple is of impressive dimensions completed in an unbelievably short duration of six months due to the ceaseless effort of ten thousand artisans, four thousand chief masons along with a hundred elephants. It is a rectangular corridor fully open at the sides and covered on top with huge granite slabs running all along the four directions.

Three hundred and sixty-five (two other versions too exist) majestic pillars and one fourth in memory of the master craftsman support the entire structure. Each pillar has a *Dīpalakṣmī* (female figure carrying a lamp in her cupped hands) facing the *Seevelippura.* The other three sides are engraved with figures of Gods, men, animals, floral designs, etc., surprisingly the ornamentation of no two pillars are identical, each is entirely different from the other. On the ceiling of the *Seevelippura* are often chiseled the fish, mainly the *Makara Matsyam,* auspicious one in the Vaishnavite faith, the sacred counch (*Śaṅkha*), wheel (*Cakra*), and so on. The massive structure running the entire outer area of the shrine is a continuous corridor primarily used for the *Śrībali* (ceremonial circumambulation of the deities) procession. It could accommodate two thousand people at a time and collective prayers and mass food distribution etc. were conducted along the corridor.

On proceeding southwards from the spot of the flagstaff, immediately on the western inner area rests the famed Kulaśekhara *Maṇḍapa* moving along the eastern corridor on the left, touching the boundary wall is a covered pillared structure, an area earmarked for the officials and families to watch the processions. Further on is a comparatively narrow corridor to the left, going eastwards with pillars representing the *Daśāvatāras,* at the end of this is a private entrance used by the Mahārājā and members of the royal family and is known as 'Chempakathumoodu Naṭa'.

Each of the four corners of the temple has a *Maṇḍapa* popularly known as the Unjal *Maṇḍapam,* with an elevated platform carved with figurines. These are used for special events and also act as platforms for presenting temple arts, discourses and discussions. The first Unjal *Maṇḍapam* is situated in the south-eastern corner. Near it touching the southern wall are situated to tiled buildings, one containing the personal *pūjā* deities of the then Maharaja Śrī Chithira Tirunal enclosed in an wooden temple replica. The other part is the *Homappura* to conduct the Mahāgaṇapati *homa.* Adjacent to this are two granite pillars for the *Tulābhāram* or weighing a person against the commodity specified to the deity, the expensive *Tulāpuruṣa Dānam* were in the kings were weighed against gold coins, that was an inevitable ritual to be performed before assuming the title of 'Kulashekara Perumal'.

The Bhadradeepappura or Deepayaga *Maṇḍapam* is situated on the western side of these pillars and is enclosed within another wall. The ancient structure is fashioned in Kerala architectural style that houses a *śālagrāma* of great potency. The temple well comes next, on the opposite side of which is the big kitchen or *Valiya Madapalli* for large scale cooking and houses the offices of the Chief Officer/ *Śrīkaryakkar* and Deputy Officer, responsible for the daily administration of the temple.

On the central right of the corridor is situated the centuries old Śrī Dharma Sastha Shrine at the *Kanni Moola* (south-west corner). The shrine being circular in shape tapers towards the top carrying numerous celestial figures and figurines sculptured beautifully. The outer wall is covered with wooden frames carrying lamp holders. Interior walls of the shrine possess traces of once elegant murals.

Taking the western path after the second Unjal *Maṇḍapam* on the central portion of the corridor facing the western entrance is a sacred place in itself.(It is here the second *Dīpārādhana* is conducted during the famed *Alpasi* and *Painkunni* festivals of the temple are conducted and the *vāhana* (vehicle) of Śrī Kṛṣṇa joins the procession at this juncture. Apart from this it is believed that the *Syamantaka* gem of the Śrī Kṛṣṇa fame is buried here. The western entrance is double-storied unlike the north and the south, and houses the *Granthappura* or the record room of the numerous manuscripts/*churunas*(or palm leaf scrolls, the temple contains about three lakh manuscripts, the largest collection in Asia) related to the day today practices and administration of the temple.

Passing on to the corner of the western corridor where it meets the northern is located another small entrance, specially used for the royal ladies to enter and has a room inside with a wooden fretwork frontage reserved for them to watch the processions and rituals. The entrance is named *Śrīpadam Naṭa*.

Moving ahead along the northern corridor, passing on the right is the Tiru Ampati Śrī Kṛṣṇa Temple. The Śrī Kṛṣṇa shrine is the oldest structure in the temple complex and possesses an unique position of its own. The complex has its own *Dhvajastambha* and *Belikkal* (sacrificial stone) marking its extraordinary position.The magnificient carved wooden *Namaskāra-maṇḍapam* or front covered platform, is self-imposing with its entrancing work and catch hold of any vision.

On the either sides of entrance to the Śrī Kṛṣṇa Temple are two *Dvārapālakas.* Entering the temple directly in the front is the stone idol of Śrī Kṛṣṇa portrayed as Pārthasārathi. A *sopānam* leading down on the centre of which is located a small *Belikkal.* The exterior walls of the inner shrine are adorned with rich collections of murals at the zenith of its beauty, depicting the instances from Kṛṣṇa's life. The either portions of the sanctum sanctorum is a large space, once believed to have housed a cow-shed/ *Goṣālā.* The shrine therefore also known as the *Gośālā* Śrī Kṛṣṇa Temple (the Kṛṣṇa of the cow shed). The walls also possess ancient inscriptions related to the temple.

On the northern side of this corridor range a long line of buildings serving different purposes. Just right of this is the two-roomed small shrine dedicated to Kṣetrapāla and Gaṇapati nearby. The shrine also possesses murals and carving on its roof. Moving ahead of this to the left, the lofty kitchen and halls utilized for the purpose of massive free food distribution are located. At the north-eastern corner a covered veranda leads to the shrine of *Agraśālā* Gaṇapati. The first portion of the structure contains a massive wooden box-like room or *Ara,* in which paddy were stored for temple purposes. In the interior of the second portion is located a not so old consecration of Gaṇapati. Outside of this shrine is located a granite well from which water was taken for temple purposes.

Adjacent to it is located the fourth Unjal *Maṇḍapam.* At the centre of the eastern corridor we reach the initial position where the journey around the temple commenced. On the right is located the *Dhvajastambha*, the hall of sculptures,the *Belikkal* area and the main entrance to the inner temple complex or the *nalambalam.*

Moving ahead of the Golden flagstaff is located the area called the 'hall of sculptures' at the centre of which, the *Valia Belikkal* is located. This is a double hall abounded with pillars offering endless fascination. By and large the sculptures follow the patterns laid down in the *Śilparatnam, Syanandūra-Purāṇa-samuchayam, Īśānaśivagurudevapaddhati* being the authoritative works. The centre of this hall is consecrated the main *Belikkal* in granite and gold plated. On the ceiling of it is pictured an aesthetically carved lotus from which is suspended a chain made of stone, probably a bell was hung earlier. The pillars around these marvelous pieces on which adorns numerous life throbbing sculptures of deities. Sculptures of Dakṣa, Śrī Rāma, Lakṣmaṇa, Sītā, dancing Śiva, Bhikṣāṭana Śiva, Rati and Kāmadeva, Ūrdhva Tāṇḍavam, Gajendra Mokṣam, Dvārapālakas, etc. The two pillars having life size statues of Hanumān and Aṣṭāṅga Garuḍa are remarkably wondrous. Between the ceiling of these two pillars is carved a complete *Meru Cakram,* with the figure of goddess Lakṣmī on either side of it. The huge main entrance door finely carved in wood, executed in Vijayanagara style lead to the interior area leading to the main shrine called the *Nalambalam.* Through this doorway is visible the sanctum sanctorum directly. There are three doorways in the inner enclosure. Stepping into the broad passage way known as the *Edanazhi* which is flanked by two large raised platforms known as *Vathil Madoms*; where the Brahmins sit and chant Vedas and other texts. The platforms on either sides are pillared and ceilings are decorated with carvings of Bhīṣma, Śiva, Garuḍa, Anantaśayana, Hanumān, Rāma, Gaṇapati, Venugopāla, Bali-Sugrīva, the Pāṇḍavas and dancing ladies, etc. Just before the Abhisravaṇa *Maṇḍapa,* a square platform comes right in front and aligns itself with the central door of the main sanctum. The *Maṇḍapa* is pillared in each corners possessing a *Dīpalakṣmī.*

'The Abhisravaṇa *Maṇḍapa* is approached by three steps each on its front and either sides. The *Maṇḍapa* possesses twelve pillars. Five of them exhibit exceptionally sculptured figures of the five Paṇḍava brothers. The *Maṇḍapa* is two storied or *dvitala.* While the three sides are open, the western side is partitioned off by wooden screens, yet one could get a glimpse of the inner shrine through the small window/door at its centre. Recanting a little, on the left of the Abhisravaṇa *Maṇḍapa* is situated the smaller kitchen where the *naivedyas* (food offerings) for the deities are prepared. And it is here that the inner southern gate is located.

Just right of this is situated the shrine of the second main deity, Śrī Narasiṃha Swamy. The *sopānam* (flight of Steps) leads to the two-roomed shrine of this fierceful deity possessing extraordinary powers. The consecration of Narasiṃha Swamy is of *Ugra-mūrti,* and is made of *pañcaloha.* The exterior of the shrine is filled with mural paintings.

Adjacent to the Narasiṃha Swamy shrine on its left another enclosure stands with three doors, two massive doors facing the south and the north including the small double door facing the *Maṇḍapa.* This is the *Cheruchuttu* which is the immediate surrounding area of the sanctum sanctorum. Entering the inner area, on its middle is the famed platform of one single granite called the Ottakkal *Maṇḍapa* or the Ekśīlā *Maṇḍapa,* built during the time of Marthanda Varma in AD 1731. The *Maṇḍapa* is of a single massive granite quarried from Tirumala in the outskirts of the city and carried all the way through with the effort of numerous workers. It measures about 18x18 feet and 12 ´feet thick. Fourteen finely carved pillars covered in gold adorn the *Maṇḍapa.* The ceiling of which is elegant with imposing carvings of *Aṣṭadikpālakas* in nine panels, with Brahmā at the centre.

This is another unique feature of this temple that, compared to other Kerala type temples the *sopāna* or the flight of steps from the small front platform immediately outside the sanctum is absent and is replaced with the Ottakkal *Maṇḍapa* as a continuation to the sanctum.

Three sets of doors open to it from the sanctum. Two *Dvārapālakas* of massive size are carved guarding either sides of the middle doors. The three doors are finely carved, plated with brass, copper and zinc alloy, and decorated with figurines of the Varāha, Kṛṣṇa, Hanumān, etc. on the first, Gaṇapati, Śiva, Viṣṇu, Lakṣmī, Garuḍa on the second and Anantaśāyī, Gaṇapati, Kāliyamardana, Śiva-Pārvati, etc. along with floral designs on the third door.

Beyond these doors are the *Garbhagṛha* or *Śrīkovil.* This rectangular sanctum sanctorum measures twenty-four feet long, eighteen feet wide and forty feet high. Consisting of two portions, of which the first is a long corridor type area and the second slightly elevated being the chamber where the main deity, Śrī Padmanābha Swamy is consecrated. The idol of the Lord in itself an iconographical marvel, is made up of a peculiar composition known as the *Katu-Sarkara-yogam* with 12008 sacred *Śālagrāmas* (sacred stone of great potency) brought from the Gandaki river in Nepal. The *Mūla vigraha* is eighteen feet long. The Lord is represented as in *Yoganidrā* with eyes partially shut reclining on the serpent Ananta. Brahmā seated on the lotus arising from the navel (*nābhi*) of the Lord. The raised left hand holds the lotus and below the right hand is a Śivaliṅga. The two sages Mārkaṇḍeya and Bhṛgu as well as the consorts of the Lord, Lakṣmī and Bhūmi devīs in sitting posture including other sages are seen in the *Garbhagṛha.* The *Abhiṣeka* idol in gold and the *Seeveli* idol in silver used for outer processions are also placed inside the sanctum.

The *Garbhagṛha* is two storied or *dvitala* structure with murals adorning the interior and exterior walls. The roof or *vimāna* of Dravidian style is tiled with copper sheets and has three gold *stūpikās* upon it. On the second level of the double storied construction of the sanctum in the mid portion of each side, on blocks of wood stand four figures of the *Koṣṭha Devatās* of the four directions. They include Viṣṇu (East), Brahmā (North), Narasiṃha (West) and Dakṣināmūrti/Śiva (South). The first two represent the *Sattva guṇa,* and the last two are indicative of the *Rajo* and *Tamo guṇas.* Apart from these numerous other celestials and episodes from the epics and the Purāṇas are abundantly worked.

Alighting from the single stone platform, on the left is situated the shrine of Viṣvaksena (Lord Viṣṇu himself). It is another salient feature of this particular temple that, compared to any other temples in Kerala, the peculiar position reserved for Mahāgaṇapati is replaced and is attributed to Viṣavaksena. This is a typical feature among the unusual structural or procedural changes practiced, in contrast to other temples in Kerala.

Retracting back, the northern area is reached, wherein on the right (eastern side of *Cheruchuttu*) is located the Rāma Swamy shrine. The northern gate/door is also known as *Svargavathil* or the gate to Heaven, having its own ritualistic importance.

As one emerges out of the *Cheruchuttu* through the southern entrance near the Narasiṃha Swamy shrine, to the left of the western inner corridor is the area called the 'Mahābhāratakonu' having its own peculiarity. The largest temple mural in Kerala of the Anantaśāyī Viṣṇu adorn the walls of this area. Moving forward on the southern side of the inner corridor, approached by few steps is the shrine dedicated to Veda Vyāsa and Aśvatthāman. Soon after this area on the right is seen a gold-plated window like representation on the exterior of the sanctum wall on the south, where the sacred feet point of the Lord is located. Proceeding further near to the *Svargavathil Natavar* area, a small square platform on right called the Kariva *Maṇḍapa* or Thiruvolakka *Maṇḍapa* is located. Immediately beyond this is the Alaṅkāra *Maṇḍapa* on left having finely carved motifs filling eight round pillars and twelve square pillars depicting the ten incarnations of Lord Viṣṇu. Adding to one's curiosity, sixty-four arts of ancient India have also been illustrated on the bigger pillars.On its ceiling are depicted the *Aṣṭadikpālakas* starting with Lord Śiva in the north-eastern corner.

Moving along this, on the right is the Abhiśravana *Maṇḍapa* and thus is reached the eastern corridor of the *Nalambalam*, from where the circumambulation of the inner area was set off. All around the exterior portion of the *Nalambalam*, wooden frames fixed on planks comprising of lamp holders are erected called the *Dīpaśālā* or *Vilkkumadom*, where once the entire lamps are lit provides a cosmic trance to the devotees. This structure is an attribute of Kerala temple architecture.

The structural marvel would not be complete without the details of the Kulaśekara *Maṇḍapa*.

The Kulaśekara *Maṇḍapa* is an extraordinary creation,the one being like a poetry in stone. It expresses the zenith of creativity. The *Maṇḍapa* was constructed at the order of Maharaja Karthika Tirunal Rāma Varma and completed in 1958 to perform the elaborate ritual of 'Hiraṇyagarbha' for the Maharaja who would gain the prestigious title of 'Kulaṣekara Perumal'. The style of figures are predominantly Tamil, yet typical Keralile features are also incorporated. This rectangular structure is enclosed within a framework of wooden railings .The outer boundary of which is thirty-six finely chiseled *Dīpalakṣmī* figures. The main platform is slightly elevated from the outer one and is separated by a small corridor between them.The bottom of the platform appears like an upturned lotus and is highly carved. Depicted on the granite ceiling are episodes from the Rāmāyaṇa. The main platform contains twenty eight pillars, embellished with vast variety of figures. Out of these twenty-eight, four ornamented pillars on the four corners of the Maṇḍapa are unique and are the musical pillars. Each group possesses nine pillars producing as many musical resonances and sounds of percussion instruments. This is one among the eleven such temples in India possessing such creative excellence.

Each pillar has a central figure of a deity and surrounded by numerous other deities and celestial beings along with elaborate designs. To delineate each one here demands more space and is perilous; henceforth some of the depictions are mentioned. The sculptures decorating the pillars includes that of Śiva-Śakti Pañcākṣarī, Dhyāna Mahā-Viṣṇu, Svayamvara Śiva with Viṣṇu, Brahmā and Hanumān, Mahāgāyatrī, Mahālakṣmī Gopāla, Ananthaśāyīmūrti-Viṣṇu seated on Ananta frankled by Grauḍa and Hanumān, Svayamvara Rukmiṇī, Veṇugopāla, Viṣṇu, Lord anointing himself with *Amṛtābhiṣeka* (nectar), Vīra Rāma, Caturbāhu Gaṇapati, Brahmāṇḍa-tāṇḍavamūrti, Svayamvara Śrī Kṛṣṇa, Śrī Rāma Paṭṭābhiṣeka, Gajendramokṣa, Svayamvara Padmāvtī, Bhadrakālī, Śrī Śaṅkaranārāyaṇa, etc. These elegant pieces are themselves works of art with their seductive stance and exquisite features. This *Maṇḍapa* is a source of eternal delight radiating life, providing divine *ānanda* (bliss) to the devotees and the lovers of art.The magnificence of this unique structure itself is an unparalleled attribute to the Śrī Padmanābha Swamy Temple.

This marks the complete *pradakṣiṇa* (circumambulation)of the mighty temple,peeping into the architectural marvel and divine manifestation.The architectural splendor here is symbolic with the attribute of Lord Viṣṇu as '*Alaṅkārapriya*' or one fond of ornamentation and hence the abode of the one 'Supreme' is expressive with artistic excellence and craftsmanship, in addition to its several salient features that Śrī Padmanābha Swamy Temple alone possesses.

The potential and divinity of the Śrī Padmanābha Swamy Temple is renowned world over since its inception. With the recent revelations of the invaluable treasure, the temple has gained world-wide fame. Though the value of these ancient riches are yet to be determined, the glory of the temple has crossed borders and captured lasting position in the minds of the people around the world. Substantially, the temple presents a unique architectural grandeur establishing itself in the pedestal of the South Indian Temple Architecture. It is therefore stressed, the essentiality of assimilating and appreciating this paramount creative aspect of temple architecture that has surpassed the vigorous tests of time, radiating perpetual celestial bliss.

References

Gouri Lakshmi Bayi, Aswati Tirunal, *Śrī Padmanābha Swamy Temple* (Reprint), Bharatiya Vidya Bhavan, Mumbai, 2000.

Menon, A.G, *History of Śri Padmanābhasvami Temple.*

Menon, A. Śrīdhara, *A Survey of Kerala History,* repr., S. Viswanathan Printers and Publishers, Chennai, 2003.

Nair, Adoor. K. K. Rāmachandran, *Shangoony Menon's History of Travancore,* Department of Gazateers Kerala, Thiruvananthapuram, 1983.

Pillai, T. K. Velu, *Travancore State Manual,* vol. IV, Government of Travancore, 1940.

Raja, R.P., *Surrender' Śrī Padmanābha Swamy Temple Renovation Souvenir,* Thiruvananthapuram, 2002.

Ramachandran, C K., *Kerala-Caritharam,* vol. II, Kerala History Association, Ernakulam, 1974.

Retnamma, K., *Ananthapuravarnanam* (Mal.), State Institute of Languages, Kerala, Thiruvananthapuram, 1997.

Sasibhushan, M.G., *Keralathile Chuvarchitrangal* (Mal.), State Institute of Languages, Kerala, Thiruvananthapuram, 2011.

Srinivasan, K.R., *Temples of South India,* reprint, National Book Trust, New Delhi, 2008.

13

IMPORTANCE OF THE TECHNIQUES OF VĀSTU LAKṢAṆA IN THE MODERN HOUSE CONSTRUCTION: AN ANALYSIS

GOPAKUMAR A.

Constructing a house is the dream of every person. Usually people construct houses according to their needs and subject to their financial capacity. But many people are not bothered about the importance of land and environment in construction of a dwelling house. It is true that due to the rapid urbanisation and modernisation it seems difficult to consider all the environmental and land factors. The non-availability of authoritative books which explains the selection of environment and land for constructing a house is also another big problem.

This paper is prepared in accordance with the book the '*Vāstulakṣaṇam*' written by Shri Ramanunni Shastri, which is preserved in the Manuscripts Library, University of Kerala. This paper describes the importance of modern architecture. This paper also attempts to answer how to construct houses which can overcome any type of climate change and other hazards. This book describes suitable and unsuitable land for living. It also includes selection of land on the basis of Cāturvarṇya. Other than these it inculcates land division and path division. It gives detailed description on installation of idols of gods, utilisation of each rooms, and the methods of establishment of Thazhikakkudam and construction of ceiling and wooden frames for door.

This book describes first the nature of land which is

suitable for house construction. The land which is low in east side and high in western side should be selected. This land should be filled with human beings and cows. The land should be suitable for all types of trees. The land should have brook and river which flows on the right side of the house. In such a place river should carry water even in summer season. Here climatic condition should be stable even in winter and monsoon seasons. Such a land is suitable for construction of houses.

This book describes the land which is not suitable for house construction. The land having corners two, three, five, six as well as having corners like crescent shaped is not suitable for house construction. The land having ashes, skelton, hair, graveyard, snake, worms, rat, pig, fox, bad odour, etc. is also not suitable.

In Cāturvarṇya society has been divided into four, such as Brahmins, Kṣatriyas, Vaiśyas and Śūdras. According to this division the land for house construction has also been fixed. The land having a square shape, white-coloured, ghee smelled, tasty was allotted to the Brahmins. The land having one eighth length, red colour, blood smelled, bitter tasted was allotted to Kṣatriyas. The land having one-sixth length, with bushes, yellow coloured, food smelled was allotted to the Vaiśyas. The land having one-fourth in length, black coloured, liquor smelled was allotted to the Śūdras.

For identifying the suitable land in accordance with the *cāturvarṇya* system, first step was to dig a pit on the land. A lamp is lighted with a prayer to Brahmā. Then the direction of the flame will be identified. If it is in the eastern direction, it should be allotted to the Brahmins, if it is west, it is to the Vaiśyas, if it was north, it is to Śūdra, if it is to south, it is to Kṣatriyas.

When the land is selected, it is divided into four parts. 1. Īśāna *koṇa* (north-east), 2. Agni *koṇa* (south-east), 3. Nirṛti *koṇa* (south-west), 4. Vāyu *koṇa* (north-west). Among these, Īśāna *koṇa* is prescribed for the house construction.

Then this book describes the methods of dividing land into nine *vīthis* to find out which are suitable for human life and which are not. The path which is suitable for living are called as Deva *vīthi,* Vaiśravaṇa *vīthi,* Varuṇa *vīthi,* Vighneśvara *vīthi,* and Brahmā *vīthi.* In all these paths, all castes such as Brāhmaṇa, Kṣatriya, Vaiśya and Śūdra can build houses. Four *vīthis* are not suitable for house construction, such as 1. Yama *vīthi,* 2. Agni *vīthi,* 3. Nāga *vīthi,* 4. Paiśāca *vīthi.*

The land which has a high western side and a low eastern side and a water flow towards eastern side is called as *Govīthi.* This is also suitable for house construction. A land having a high Vāyu *koṇa* and a low Agni *koṇa* with water flow towards that kon is called a Agni *vīthi.* A land having a high northern side and a low southern side with water flowing toward south is called as Yama *vīthi.*

In this land the idols of gods will be installed in each corners. In easten side Jayanta, Indra, Āditya, Satyaka, Antarīkṣaka and Dṛśa will be installed. In southern side, the idols of Vidadhar, Mṛga, Dvāraka will be installed. Moreover in the south, Varuṇa, Vāyudeva and Vivasvān In south west side Mitra will be installed. In the northern side maheedharan, in the Īśāna *koṇa* (north-east) Āpa and Āpavalsa, in Agni *koṇa,* Saviyhav and Sāvitra and other *koṇas* Indra and Indrajaya, in Vāyu *koṇa* Rudra and Rudrajaya will be installed. Inside at the right central part Brahmā also will be installed.

Along with all these topics, the book describes the needs and uses of each room. The room at the eastern side is used for fire ceremony, god ceremony, sacrifice ceremony. The rooms in the northern side are used for the women and children and the Brahmin women lived in the eastern room. The room at the south side are used for the guests. Dharma Goddesses' ceremony is conducted in this room itself. The western room is used for collecting and keeping wealth and treasure. The excess rooms are used for the study and sleeping. Rooms in the Nirṛti *koṇa* (south-west) are used for preparing food and its consumptions.

A pond has to be built up in the *Indrapatha* (eastern side) or *Varuṇapatha* (western side). The kitchen should be built in *Agnipatha* (south-east). The Oottupura (dining hall) should be built in front of the kitchen. The well has to be built near the dining hall and kitchen. Besides this the store room should be built near the kitchen and dining hall. The paddy should be stored in the Nirṛti *koṇa* (south-west). The cow shed should be built up in the *Varuṇapatha* (west).

Maṇḍapaśālā, for the sitting of king and Brāhmaṇas, should be built in central portion and this place can also be used for ceremonies and worship and for receiving guests. The next step describes how to find out strong and pure land. If a path is there in between both lands no faults will come to others. The next step describe the installation of Thazhika kudam in the house. It is installed in the ceiling being constructed by polished *kazhukkol*. Thazhika kudam is covered by a round of iron strip. It must have a *pañca kumbhādi*. Its end must be like lotus buds. Its upper portion must be built by strong metals like copper, silver etc. having the resistance power against rain, sunlight, wind and fog.

The next portion describes the construction of ceiling and how to make strong pillars etc. This paper is an attempt to explain the knowledge of indigenous Indian architecture and its usage in modern house construction.

14

JEWISH ARCHITECTURE: THE CONCEPT OF HEBRAIC SHRINES THROUGH THE AGES

JENUSHA. K.S.

Every religion has associated with it a shrine of some sort or the other. The nature of the shrine varies according to the religion it is associated with, as also its symbolism is perceived differently in each religion. As far as Judaic shrines are concerned, they are the ones belonging to a most ancient tradition that is still to be observed. At present, the Jewish religious institution is the Synagogue. And it has been so for over two millennia now. And yet, it is a fact that a decentralized religious institution like the Synagogue was not the original concept in Judaism as far as a monument of worship was concerned. At the core of Judaism, the concept of religious institution was a centralized one—first in the form of the Tabernacle of Moses, and later as the Temple of Solomon at Jerusalem the relics of which still remain. The concept of Synagogue originated even later, as a consequence, quite strangely, not of any religious developments, but rather due to the socio-political ramifications of the times. The present study is an attempt to trace this development of Hebraic shrines from the Tabernacle to the Synagogue.

"Like every other object of human enquiry, Architecture may be studied from two distinct points of view. Either it may be regarded statically, and described scientifically as a thing existing, without any reference to the manner in which it was invented; or it may be treated historically, tracing every form from its origin, and noting the influence one style has had upon another in the progress of time."—James Fergusson (*Encyclopaedia of World Architecture: From the Earliest to the Present Times*, vol.1).

This study is an enquiry from the second mentioned perspective; for, taking a case study, it looks at the development, or rather transformation the architectural concept of a religious institution has undergone over time. Here the case, as mentioned in the title, is of the shrines in Judaism. As you all may well be aware, Synagogue is the religious institution, the place of worship, for the Jews. And yet, in this enquiry, I am not searching for traces of development of Synagogues; simply because of the fact that, as far as Judaism is concerned, Synagogue has not always been the holy shrine. In fact, considering the very deep antiquity of the religion, Synagogue is a relatively later, much later institution.

Let us look at the beginnings now. Though material or archaeological evidences are lacking for such shrines of the ancient past, there are vivid literary references which occur mostly in the very scripture the Jews themselves adhere to, namely the *Torah*. The other literary sources include the writings of the early century writers, Philo of Alexandria and Josephus.

Regarding the shrines referred to in the scripture, the first significant one is the Tabernacle built by Moses during his wanderings in Mt. Sinai. There are, of course, references to altars erected even before the time of Moses. Noah, Abraham, Jacob and others have set up altars at various times in various places. But there is no detailed account of such altars, other than just the mention of them being erected.

The first detailed account of a shrine comes in the *Exodus* which relates to the building up of the Tabernacle upon the command of God who instructs Moses giving precise information regarding the measurements, the plan and such objects as the seven-branched candle stand (*menorah*), the table for Unleavened Bread, and so on. And accordingly, the shrine was erected and was known as the Tent of the Lord's Presence. In the Tent was kept the Commandment-Tablets in a chest known as the *Ark of the Covenant*, in the Most Holy Place which is separated by the Holy Place by a curtain. Another chief feature of the Tabernacle was the sacrificial altar.

The next significant shrine mentioned in the scripture is the Temple of Solomon in Jerusalem of which only the portion of a fortified wall remains known as the Wailing Wall. The Temple was built not in accordance with the measurements used in the Tabernacle, but made splendid and enlarged in proportion, in accordance with the king's might and wealth; though the basic plan conformed to that of the Tabernacle, with the interior division into three parts, viz. a porch (*ulam*), a sanctuary (*hechal*) and the Holy of Holies (*debir*); just like the porch, the Holy Place and the Most Holy Place of Moses' Tent. The Temple was destroyed and reconstructed several times and during each phase; various cultures had their influence on the Temple architecture and art; until its final devastation by the Roman Titus in AD 70. Nevertheless, this Temple became more renowned and significant than the Tabernacle.

In the case of a Synagogue, there are no literary references concerning its architecture during the beginning stages. Its origin and development must be traced from the historical milieu, the socio-political developments of the times triggering the transformation in the mode of worship amongst the Jews.

During the Babylonian invasion of Jerusalem in 586 BC, many Jews were exiled to Babylon. This made it impossible for these Jews to continue their worship in the Temple and they found themselves secluded amidst the belief system of the new place. Many of them gathered together to pray and read the *Torah*, to make amends for their inability to go to the Temple and as a way to hold on to their faith in whatever way possible. Prophets like Ezra and other scholars of the scripture preached that it is not necessary that one should go to the Temple, for the Lord dwells in one's heart and it would do to believe in the One and hold on to the commandments in the scripture and keep up the Covenant wherever one is.

The Jews, thus, began to gather and read the *Torah* and this became their chief mode of worship. Many scholars consider these assembly halls to be the beginning of Synagogues. And these were only simple chambers or houses meant for the purpose without any regulation regarding the plan or architectural features. Besides the reading of the *Torah*, matters of religious importance began to be discussed in these gatherings. Later, when Jerusalem came under the rule of the Persians, the Jews were allowed to return and the ones who came back continued the mode of worship they had practised while in exile. Besides, many of these Jews lived far away from the Temple that it was still difficult for them to go there for daily worship. Hence, as in the land of exile, assemblies began to be held in the homeland too. Thus, side by side with the worship at the Temple, that at Synagogues, too, began to gain importance. The Jews, however, used to make pilgrimages to the Temple, at times.

With the total destruction of the Temple in 70 AD Synagogues began to be more and more popular and increased in number. And yet, none of them ever had the position the Temple once had, as is evident from the importance Jews give to the Wailing Wall and the pilgrimage they make, from various parts of the world, to pray and mourn for the loss of the Temple. In a way, the Synagogues helped to reorganize the religious and social life of Jews and to safeguard their spiritual heritage, even after the fall of Jerusalem and its Temple.

Regarding literary references for Synagogues, nowhere in the Old Testament, the term is used for any institution; while in the New Testament, mention of Synagogues can be found in numerous places. There are references to Synagogues at Capernaum, Galilee, Jericho, Nazareth, and other places in and around the present Israel-Palestine region. Excavations in the Biblical lands have also revealed structures ascribed to as Synagogues – at Masada, Herodium, Gamla, Baram, Dura-Europos etc. Obviously, by the 1st Century AD, the Synagogues had become well established religious institutions. And later, as the Jews began to spread into various parts of the world, Synagogues began to be established in those places too.

The Synagogues, in general, have an Ark placed in or near the wall facing the direction of Jerusalem, in which the *Torah* scrolls are kept and which is covered by a curtain known as the *parokhet*; and a pulpit, though placed in the centre traditionally, can be found variously placed in different Synagogues. The *Ner Tamid* or the Eternal Lamp is lit in all Synagogues. The Synagogues have separate galleries for women the placement of which also differs.

In spite of the fact that there had been numerous Synagogues, as indicated by the literary and archaeological evidences, there is hardly any homogeneity or universality in the Synagogue architecture. The reason for this can be found in the disturbed history of Jews who were most often in exile in various lands. The architecture of any form develops when there is a prolonged settlement at a particular place which never happened with the Jewish communities. Even in their homeland, they very frequently faced social, political and religious chaos that such aspects as art and architecture adopted kept changing in accordance with time and circumstance.

The Synagogues which began to be set up in various

countries, adopted the architectural features of the native local tradition. As such, Synagogues of various places are far different from one another. Also, the Synagogues belonging to various sects like the Sephardim and Ashkenazim also differ.

The excavations reveal Synagogues of various kinds having different plans. The larger ones were colonnaded with the hall being divided into nave and aisle by the supporting columns. Almost all Synagogues seem to have had the main chamber and the porch in front of it and the pulpit in the centre of the sanctuary. Benches were arranged lining the walls. And though no arks were recovered, images on mosaic floors or walls show them to be double-doored chests over which a curtain was hung.

As obvious from these descriptions, the Synagogue, the Temple and the Tabernacle, though belong to the Hebraic tradition; differ in many respects; not only in architecture, but also in the mode of worship. A community house, Synagogue serves not as a place of worship alone, but as one of assembly and study as well. It is the centre of the Jewish religious and social life. And regarding architecture too, its beginnings show that the 'gathering' was more important than the 'structure'; worship could be conducted as far as there is a quorum known as the *minyan*, i.e. the presence of at least ten males above the age of thirteen.

The Synagogues did adopt some element of the old tradition, the chief of them being the importance given to the Ark. The earlier Synagogues seem to have had portable chests like the original Ark of the Covenant, while the later arks were fixed ones inserted into the Synagogue wall facing Jerusalem as are found in the present Synagogues, too. In the place of the inscribed Commandment-Tablets, *Torah* scrolls of parchment are kept in the arks. Other objects, like the *menorah*, for instance, of the Tabernacle times are still kept. The pulpit or the reading desk was a new feature in the Synagogue. The prophet Ezra is said to have been the one who first used a raised platform from where the *Torah* was read. The arrangement of the ark, the pulpit and the porch in front of the sanctuary in the Synagogue in a vertical axis is also akin to the tripardite division of the older tradition.

Most architectural forms evolve from the simple to the complex, passing through several phases; keep adding on various elements in each, before eventually culminating in its final stage, from whence it stops its development. The Hindu temple had its structural beginning in a single cell, to which the *ardhamaṇḍapa* was added, attached to it, which got detached from it at a later stage forming a separate maṇḍapa, meanwhile adding on other elements as well, to finally form the *pañcaprākāra.* The Buddhist Stūpa, likewise developed from a simple mound to the evolved ones as seen at Sanchi, Sarnath, etc., complete with the *toraṇas, harmikā, catra,* and the circumambulatory passages. And so in almost all forms of architecture. In the case of Hebraic shrines, however, there has not exactly been an evolution from the simple to the complex. It has been a change in other ways, as evident from the descriptions of details explained here. The transformation is not simply architectural alone; but is also conceptual/ideological; as well as functional. In fact, the transformation in architecture is because and as a result of the conceptual transformation behind it. The focus of the Tabernacle worship was the sacrifice and there was an altar for that. There also existed segregation; for, only the High Priest could enter the Most Holy Place. More or less similar is the case of the Temple. And both the Tabernacle and the Temple were centralized institutions, each being the only one of its kind. The Synagogues, on the other hand, far differ from these. Synagogues are not centralized shrines, but could be established anywhere. And, as stated earlier, they served in the form of assemblies, having no segregation among the groups. The reading of the *Torah* became the main service and sacrifice was altogether abandoned.

The development of Hebraic shrines, from the Tabernacle to the Synagogue, is also indicative of the socio-cultural milieu of the times. Culture is dynamic, and its many vagaries are reflected in its various facets, be it is in literature, art, or architecture. And the story of the Hebraic shrines is a testimony to this.

Bibliography

1. Abramovitz, Max. *Synagogues in Forms and Functions of Twentieth Century Architecture* (ed). Talbot Hamlin. New York: Columbia University Press, 1952.
2. *Encyclopaedia of Religion,* vol.14 (ed). Mircea Eliade. New York: Macmillan, 1987.
3. Farrington, Karen. *Hamlyn History Religion.* London: Reed Consumer Book Limited, 1998.
4. *Good News Bible.* The Bible Society of India. Bangalore, 2005.
5. Hachili, Rachel. *The Archaeology of Judaism* in *Archaeology and World Religion*(ed). Timothy Insoll. London: Routledge, 2001.
6. *New Encyclopaedia Britannica,* vol. 22. U.S.A., 2005.
7. *Oxford Companion to the Bible*(ed). Bruce M. Metzger and Michael D. Coogan. London: Random House, 1999.
8. Snell, Heber Cyrus. *Ancient Israel: Its Story and Meaning.* New York: Stevens and Wallis, 1948.
9. www.jewishencyclopaedia.com.

15

CONSTRUCTION OF PLAYHOUSE IN THE NĀṬYAŚĀSTRA

Renjith Rajan

The term 'architecture' means, the art or science of designing and constructing buildings and other physical structures. Indian architecture is as old as the history of civilization. The earliest remains of recognizable building activity in India dates back to the Indus Valley cities. Among India's ancient architectural remains, the most characteristic are the temples, caityas, vihāras, stūpas and other religious structures. In ancient India, temple architecture of high standard developed in almost all regions. The distinct architectural style of temple construction in different parts was a result of geographical, climatic, racial, historical and linguistic diversities. Ancient Indian temples have a hall to present the art forms which is known as *Nāṭyamaṇḍapa* or play house because the temples serve an important part in the development of dramas. The hall is considered to be as sacred as the temple sanctum itself.

References to architecture are found in ancient literatures like the Vedas (Ṛgveda, Yajurveda, Sāmaveda, Atharvaveda) and Sthāpatyaveda, an Upaveda of Atharvaveda. Ancient literature has the references and knowledge about construction of buildings from houses to forts, palaces, temples and *yajñaśālās*. Lord Buddha is supposed to have given instructions to his disciples about the construction of Vihāras.

The *Nāṭyaśāstra* of sage Bharata, the first work on drāma and dramaturgy, belongs to the second century BC. In this work the author deals with all the aspects of a drama. The treatise has thirty-six chapters. Minute aspects of a drama are depicted there in detail. After the description of the origin of drāma Bharata pays first importance in the description of play house or *Nāṭyamaṇḍapa*. A *Nāṭyamaṇḍapa* is an integral part in the staging of a drama. Presentation of a drama is not that much effective without a play house. So Bharata, the master of dramaturgy gives ample space in the description of playhouse.

In the first chapter he describes the incident, which led to the formation of the first *Nāṭyamaṇḍapa*. At first in the Indradhvaja festival, the play *Amṛtamanthana* was presented without a *Nāṭyamaṇḍapa*. All of the spectators were pleased and eager to watch the drama. But when the performance relating to the killing of the Daityas and Dānavas began, the Daityas who came there instigated by the Vighnas with Asuras paralysed the speech movement as well as memory of the actors. Then Indra took the banner staff and smashed the Vighnas and Asuras. After the incident Bharata along with the Devas approached Brahmā and asked him to enlighten him on the means of the protection of the drama. Hearing that Brahmā asked Viśvakarman to build a playhouse of best type to protect drama from the Vighnas and Asuras. Thus he created the playhouse.

Then in the second chapter *Prekṣāgṛhalakṣaṇa*, Bharata provides valuable information on domestic architecture and the construction of a playhouse in detail. He says that Viśvakarman devised three types of theatres according to the Śāstras, viz. vikṛṣṭa, i.e., rectangular, *caturasra*, i.e. square, and *tryasra*, i.e., triangular. Each of these three again falls into three kinds according to size: *jyeṣṭha,* i.e. biggest, *madhyama,* i.e. middle-sized; and *kaniyas,* i.e., small. Of these three, Bharata asks to choose the middle-sized for the best visual and audio effect. A reading of the verses here would give the idea that the biggest is for the Devas, the middle-sized for kings, and the small for the people. Abhinava's commentary here gives original interpretation, that if Bharata assigns the biggest theatre to the Devas, it means that the people who present the drama should resort to the biggest to enact such kinds of dramas as the *Ḍima* in which occur fights between the Devas and the Asuras and consequently much space is wanted. If the romances of a king's private life have to be enacted, the middle-sized theatre is enough for this purpose and must go to the small theatre when the monologue, *Bhāna* plays in which ordinary men and women are characters. Bharata asks mortals not to compete with the very big theatres of Devas because mortals must build with great trouble while they do things by mere wish. Bharata recommends the middle-sized theatre to the mortals.

General instructions

Bharata states so many steps in accordance with the construction of a playhouse. He describes so many ceremonial functions also in each step in accordance with the construction of a playhouse such as *dānakarma* of various things like jewels, cloth, food, cow, etc. to the Brahmins. The first step is the selection of a suitable site. The preparation of the plot described there in detail. He says that an expert builder should, first of all, examine a plot of land and then proceed with a good resolve to measure the site. A playhouse should be erected on a soil which is plain, firm, hard and black and not white. It should first of all be cleared and then scratched with a plough; and then bones potsherds as well as grass and shrubs growing in it, are to be removed. The ground after being cleared should be measured out with a piece of white string which may be made of cotton, wool, *muñja* grass or bark of tree.

Vikṛṣṭa

After this the builder should measure a plot of land 64 *hasta* long and divide the same into two equal parts. The back portion will be divided again into two equal halves. Of these the back portion should be again divided equally into two parts, and one of these halves will be made the *raṅgaśīrṣa* and on the part at the back the *nepathya*.

Having divided the plot of the land he should lay in it the foundation of the playhouse, with the assistance of the sounds of musical instruments like *śaṅkha, dundubhi, paṇava,* etc. After laying the foundation, the pillars of the play house have to be raised. Bharata makes rules on this. He dedicates four main pillars to the four castes even as portions of the whole theatre to the various gods for the sake of protection. Then he comments on the construction of *Mattavāraṇī,* the floor which is prepared on both sides of the *Raṅgapīṭha.* This should be furnished with four pillars and should be equal in length to the stage and its height should be one and a half *hasta.* The *Raṅgamaṇḍapa* should be equal in height to that of the two Mattavāraṇī-s. After this the *Raṅgapīṭha* should be constructed. In the construction of the *Raṅgapīṭha* Bharata primarily gives notes on the construction of *raṅgaśīrṣa* or the stage. The *raṅgaśīrṣa* should include six pieces of wood. Here it is that the actors make offerings and *pūjā* before the drama begins and wait during the drama when they have dressed themselves up. Abhinava says that if the stage is imagined as a man lying on his back, this space called the *raṅgaśīrṣa* will look like his head. The *nepathya* or the trying room should be furnished with two doors. While filling up the ground marked for the *raṅgaśīrṣa* the black soil should be used with great care. The earth is to be made free from stone chips, gravel and grass by the use of a plough, to which are to be yoked two white draught animals. The interesting thing there instructed by Bharata is that who should be employed in the job. He strictly instructs that the employees should be free from physical difficulties of all kind. The surface of the *Raṅgapīṭha* should not be like the *Kūrmapṛṣṭha* (high at the centre and sloping on all-sides like the back of a tortoise), or the Matsyapṛṣṭha (high along the centre and sloping on both sides like the back of a fish). It should be smooth like the surface of a mirror.

The playhouse should be made like a mountain cave and it should have two floors on two different levels and small windows and it should be free from wind and should have good acoustic quality. The erection of the walls is then described. The whole hall must be richly decorated with wood-work, representing creepers, birds, animals, etc. The walls must be decorated with beautiful paintings of pictures of pleasure, of men and women and of creepers and trees, after the walls have been made smooth and white by *sudhākarma*. One should start the wood work with many artistic pieces such as decorative designs, figures of elephants, snakes, tigers, etc.

In respect of the seating arrangements also, Bharata's theatre was perfect. He says that the seating arrangements should be in the form of a gallery–*sopānākṛti*. The seats should be either of brick or of wood. They should be one and a half feet high above the ground, to give a good view of the *Raṅgapīṭha*.

Bharata paid due attention to the acoustic properties of the theatre also. He says that 64 × 32 *hastas* is the maximum size for a theatre and that one should not exceed that measurement. He praises the middle-sized one among the three kinds of houses. The reason he gives is, this: "Constructors should not build a theatre of a greater size, for the *Nāṭya* would become indistinct. If the hall should be very big, the actor's voice would either become indistinct or bad on account of the necessity for the actors to shout out.

The colour of the face or the tune of the varying *rasa* and *bhāva* would become indistinct owing to the largeness of the house. Therefore, of all halls, the middle-sized is the best, for here the instruments and songs would be heard beautifully well." Again he says that the stage should be like a cave in a mountain without very large windows, so that there might be a clear and audible sound effect. Even the windows should be fitted with aperture doors so that there might not be too much air.

Caturasra

Bharata then describes how to construct the *caturasra,* measures 32 *hastas* on both sides. In this type the *Raṅgapīṭha* is smaller naturally. The entrance to the green-room should be only one. In other respects, the construction of this type should follow the instructions given as regards to the rectangular. Just as in the rectangular type, the *Raṅgapīṭha* is also rectangular; in the square type the *Raṅgapīṭha* is square. In the rectangular the *raṅgaśīrṣa* is a little higher than the—*Raṅgapīṭha* while, in the square, both are on the same level. Its outer walls should be made with strong bricks very thickly set together. And inside the stage and in proper directions, the architect should raise ten pillars capable of supporting the roof. Outside the pillars, seats should be constructed in the form of a staircase by means of bricks and wood for the accommodation of the spectators. Successive rows of seats should be made one *hasta* higher than the floor. And all these seats should overlook the stage.

In the interior of the playhouse six more strong pillars capable of supporting the roof should be raised in suitable positions and with proper ceremonies. And in addition to these eight more pillars should be raised by their side. Then after raising *Raṅgapīṭha,* eight *hasta* square, more pillars should be raised to support the roof of the playhouse. These pillars should be properly fixed to the roof and be decorated with the figures of *śālāstrī.*

After all these have been made, one should carefully construct the *nepathya,* it should have one door leading to the *Raṅgapīṭha* through which persons should enter with their face towards the spectators. There should also be a second door facing the auditorium. The *Raṅgapīṭha* of this type should be eight *hastas* in length and in breadth. It should be furnished with an elevated *vedikā* or *Raṅgapīṭha* with plain surface. Its *Mattavāraṅī* should be made according to the measurements prescribed before. The *Mattavāraṅī* should be made with four pillars by the side of the *vedikā* of equal to it in height. In case of a playhouse of the *vikṛṣṭa* type it should be higher than the *Raṅgapīṭha,* whereas in a *caturasra* type it should have a height equal to that of *Raṅgapīṭha.*

Tryasra

Then Bharata describes a *Tryasra*—triangular theatre. The speciality to be noted in its construction is that the *Raṅgapīṭha* here is triangular and has an entrance into the green-room at its back angle. As regards the entrance gates to the audience hall, Abhinava says that they may be three, perhaps one on each side.

Concerning the size, measurement and types of theatres in general, Abhinava says that altogether eighteen kinds of theatres are possible as spoken of in the Śāstras.

Conclusion

While examining the remarks of Bharata on the making of a playhouse and employing of the workers one can understand the application of the principle of *aucitya.* He firmly suggests that the *madhyama* type of playhouse is proper one. Because the dialogues as well as the songs in it may be heard by the spectators.

Prekṣāgṛhāṇāṃ sarveṣāṃ tasmānmadhyamamiṣyate/
yasmāt pāṭhyaṃ ca geyaṃ ca sukhaṃ śrāvyataram bhavet//

II. 21

By owing the words of the *Nāṭyaśāstra* itself, we can conclude that there is no knowledge, no art or craft, no device, no action in the world that is not found in the *Nāṭyaśāstra*.

"Na tajjñānaṃ na tacchilpaṃ na sa vidyā na sa kalā
Na sa yogo na tatkarma nāṭyesmin yanna dṛśyate"

I. 116

References

1. *Nāṭyaśāstra of Bharatamuni,* trans., M.M. Ghosh, New Bharatiya Book Corporation.
2. *Bharatamuniyute Natyasastram.* trans., K.P. Narayanapisharoti.

16

ARCHITECTURE OF ANNAMALAI NADHAR MAHADEVA TEMPLE

AMBILY C.S.

Kerala lies on the south-west coast of India and is considered to be the land of temples. Kerala temples are conditioned by the zone of location, regional affiliation, the raw materials and climatic factors. Generally, the temple complex of Kerala falls under the *pañcaprākāra* scheme of architecture mentioned in the early texts. *Pañcaprākāra* denotes five enclosures around the Śrīkovil. They are: 1. Akathe Balivattom. 2. Chuttambalam. 3. Madhyahara. 4. Bāhyahara and 5. Maryādā. Temple is known as different names in different places such as *devālaya, devakula, kovil* and *mandira*. In the works of Pāṇini and Patañjali temples are mentioned as Prāsādas and the *Śatapatha-brāhmaṇa* of the period of the Vedas mentioned temple as altar. The Vedic books describe the plan of temple as square and it is divided into 64 to 81 smaller squares, where each of these represent a specific divinity.

Annamalai Nadhar Mahādeva Temple situated at Karikkode, eastern part of Thodupuzha in Idukki District of Kerala is a proud example of Kerala's rich cultural heritage. The Temple faces south which is a rare phenomenon among the temples of Kerala. It is solely constructed by using granite blocks and the *garbhagṛha* of it is rectangular in shape. The Temple is also unique in Kerala since the Temple houses about thirty-five bronze images.

Literal meaning

The literal meaning of the name of the temple is the temple of Mahādeva (Śiva), protector (Nadhar) of Annamalai. This indicates that either the place was once known as Annamalai or Śiva of this temple is the protector of a place somewhere else with the name of Annamalai.

Previous works

Unfortunately there is not much literary evidence available regarding this Temple. Though there are few articles in popular magazines and newspapers like the *Jyothishasree, Manoramā* supplement on this temple, no in-depth study, focusing on its antiquity, architecture, art, reasons for housing bronze icons and features of these icons have been done so far by any of the scholars.

Objective of the study

The present paper is an attempt to discuss the architectural features of Annamalai Nadhar Mahādeva Temple and its antiquity. For this purpose available published data and information collected from the interview of K.R. Sudhakaran (Chairman of the Annamalai Nadhar Mahadeva Temple Renovation Committee) and main features of the Temple were photo documented. The Temple is in a dilapidated condition and now in the process of getting renovated.

Legends

There are mainly three legends associated with this temple

1. *Associated with Pāṇḍyas*

The Pāṇdya Dynasty of the Middle Ages was divided into small nadus. The king ruled the dynasty as a whole at the capital and the nadus were ruled by the brothers or relatives of the king. Thus, there were nadus like Anchnadu, Kovilmalai, Arakkulam, Annamalai, etc. known far and wide. So it is believed that the ruler of the Annamalai built this temple.

2. *Associated with the Cholas*

The tradition says that the history of the Temple begins from Rājārāja and runs through Rajendra Chola, Parantham Thevan, Kovil Malayil Thevan and ends at the Maharaja of Vadakkumkoor. It is believed that there were nāṭyamaṇḍapas, dhvajas, temple prākara walls, etc. were built by famous craftsmen of that period. It is believed that this temple was one among the sixty-four temples built by the Chola rulers.

3. *Associated with a community migrated from Thenkasi*

According to this legend the granite temple was built around thirteenth century and owned by a community (Śaiva vellalas) migrated from Thenkasi.

Architecture of Annamalai Nadhar Mahādeva Temple

In Kerala, rock cut temples are considered to be the forefathers of early structural temples. The earliest evidence of structural temple dates back to the ninth century AD. Architecturally the temples of Kerala passed through three stages, they are: 1. early phase (AD 800-1000), 2. Middle phase (AD 1000-1300) and 3. Later phase (AD 1300-1500). In early phase temples were built in square, circular and apsidal plans. Oblong and rectangular plans were also in vogue. Both *sāntara* and *nirantara* temples were popular and many temples had four functional doors, conforming to the *sarvatobhadra* type. In the middle phase emergence of more than one *pradakṣiṇapatha*, the appearance of *dvitala, tritala vimāna,* detached *mukhamaṇḍapa,* etc. are the important features. In the later phase, temple architecture reaches its final stage of evolution. Emergences of multi-shrined temples, additions like *dhvajastambhas, vilakkumadam, koothambalam, theppakkalam* are the important features of this phase.

Annamalai Nadhar Mahadeva Temple has a *garbhagṛha* and an attached pillared *mukhamaṇḍapa.*

Elevation

The general features of *Śrīkovil* are *Adiṣṭhāna, Sopāna, Praṇāla,* wall or Bhitti and Roof.

1. *Adhiṣṭhāna*

Adiṣṭhāna is the basement and it has vertical moulded tiers. Tiers from bottom to top are arranged in specified order and each has specific shapes and distinct names. The *Adiṣṭhāna* of the Annamalai Nadhar Mahādeva Temple has *pādukā, jagatī, kumuda* and *gala-paṭṭi.*

2. *Vedika*

Vedī or *vedikā* is a railing and it is seen above the *Adiṣṭhāna.* The *vedikā* portion of the Annamalai Temple has *gala, padma* and *kampa* as components.

3. *Bhitti or Wall*

The *bhitti* starts from the *vedikā.* Generally the *bhitti* portion of Kerala temples is either made of granite or laterite blocks; sometimes the *bhitti* portion is plastered. In this temple it is made of granite and is without any plaster. The decorative elements seen on the wall portions are *gavākṣa, karṇakūṭa, kudhya stambha, nāsikā, pañjara, prāsāda-dvāra* and *ghana-dvāra.* There are three *ghanadvāras* seen on three side walls of the *Śrīkovil* of this temple. *Ghanadvāras* have pilasters on both sides and *toraṇas* above with *kirīṭamukha* at the top. The walls also have *gavākṣas* with *jalli* works. The *gavākṣas* on the western side wall of the *Śrīkovil* has five perforations and the eastern side has nine perforations. The jams and lower part of the main door have decorative floral elements. Some shallow depressions are seen at the base of the southern wall of the *Śrīkovil.*

4. *Roof*

The roof of the *Śrīkovil* of Kerala temple is constructed in different ways; the earliest and small temples have square granite floor. But majority of temple roofs are constructed in wood and covered with copper or terracotta tiles. The shapes varies in accordance with ground plans. In Annamalai Nadhar Mahādeva Temple, the roof is made of granite and is flat. Flat-roofed temples are rare in Kerala. At the base of the roof there are some arched niches with human faces decorating them.

5. *Praṇāla*

The *praṇāla* is an important part of the *Śrīkovil* and it is for draining out lustural water from sanctum. *Praṇāla* of various shapes,—circular, many faceted, rectangular and ornamented are noticed in Kerala temples. The *praṇāla* of this temple is seen on the northern side because the *Śrīkovil* faces south. The *praṇāla* issues from a *vyālimukha* and ends in the form of a flower. It has excellent carvings.

PLAN OF THE TEMPLE

1. *Garbhagṛha*

Garbhagṛha is the innermost part of the temple. The *Garbhagṛha* may be enclosed by an inner wall (*antar bhitti*) and an external wall (*bāhya bhitti*). The ambulatory passage in between these two walls is known as *sāntara.* In case there is no inner wall it is known as *nirantara* type. The Annamalai Nadhar Mahādeva temple is a *nirantara* type of temple. The main door of the *Garbhagṛha* faces south. It is rectangular in shape.

Pīṭha

There is a *pīṭha* at the center of the *Garbhagṛha*. Here the Śivalinga is placed. There is a platform at the back side wall in east-west orientation. This was used to place idols whilom.

2. *Mukhamaṇḍapa*

The flat-roofed *Mukhamaṇḍapa* is supported by four pillars. The central two pillars are with decorations and other two are comparatively simple. The pillars have various parts like *oma*, kāṇḍa and *pothika*. The pillars of this temple has a rectaṅgular (lower) and two square portions (middle and top).The central pillars are decorated with the images of Śiva and Parvatī, devotees flanking Śivalinga, Śāsta, sages and *Vyagrapatha*, Nāgabandha and floral decorations.

Sopāna

The approach of *Śrīkovil* is through *sopāna*. The *sopāna* of Annamalai Nadhar Mahādeva Temple is attached to the *Mukhamaṇḍapa*. It has four direct steps and balustrade with decorations on either side.

Analysis and Conclusion

Unfortunately there are not much literary evidence available regarding this temple. In his book entitled *Temples of Kerala* Jayasanker states that Annamalai Nadhar Mahādeva Temple is built in Chola style of architecture. Analysis of the architecture of this temple shows features similar to the Chola style. The peculiar early Chola style of this flat roof and pillared *Mukhamaṇḍapa* is indicative of this fact. The pillars are beautifully decorated with cut works. The *oma, kāṇḍa* and *pothika* divisions and the sculptural representation of the pillars shows similar features found in the temples of the Chola period. The entire temple is constructed using granite and the rectangular plan of the *Garbhagṛha* indicates that this is one among the temples of the early phase. Cholas established friendship with Chera kings and were engaged in matrimonial alliances. The Chola King Rājarāja Chola had matrimonial alliance with a Chera king. His wife had a habit of donating icons. This relationship might have resulted in bringing the artisans and thereby the Chola style initiated into the structures made at that time.

But according to the legend, this temple was built by Pāṇḍya kings. This may be said due to the frequent conflicts between Cholas and Pandyas. Both of them enjoyed victories every now and then. So the temple might have been built by Cholas or Cheras in Chola style and this place later believed to be under Pāṇḍyas. It is also said that the bronze work in Kerala is a heavy imitation of that which flourished in the kingdom of the Cholas. The iconographical features of bronze idols show similarities with Chola bronzes (conical *kirīṭa*, necklaces, etc.). Besides these we have strong evidence regarding the relationship between this temple and Chola kings. The *pīṭha* of the mirror with prabhā recovered from this temple is now placed in Kayamkulam Museum has an inscription, written in Tamil grantha on its stand. Though the inscription is not fully deciphered, the close observation reveals that each line of this inscription ends in a word "*cholai*". So there must be some relationship between the bronzes of this temple and Chola Dynasty. One sentence of the inscription deciphered runs like this "*Nallamukuram cheychatha cholai*" which meant the Chola built the beautiful mirror. So a member of Chola dynasty may be the person who donated the mirror, most probably as well as some idols to the temple. The name of this temple is an indicative of Tamil influence. The literal meaning indicates that either the place was once known as Annamalai or the Śiva of this temple is the protector of a place somewhere else with the name of Annamalai. There is a famous temple called Thiruvannamalai in Tamil Nadu.It was constructed by the Chola kings. All these points help to conclude that there was definitely some Chola connection to this temple. Though the exact date of the construction of this temple cannot be exactly ascertained, approximately this might have been built between tenth to eleventh century AD.

REFEERENCES

1. Ayankar, S. Krishnaswamy, *Dravidian Architecture,* Asian Educational Service, New Delhi, 1987.
2. Bernier Ronald, M., *Temple Arts of Kerala,* S. Chand, New Delhi,1982.
3. Jayasankar, S., *Temples of Kerala,* Directorate of Census Operation, Thiruvananthapuram, 1997.
4. Sarkar, H., *An Architectural Survey of Temples of Kerala,* ASI, New Delhi, 1978.
5. Soundarajan, K.V., *Temple Architecture in Kerala,* Government of Kerala,Thiruvananthapuram, 1974.
6. Tomory Edith, *Introduction to the History of Fine Arts in India and West,* Orient Longman, Madras, 1968.

17

KERALA'S CONTRIBUTION TO ARCHITECTURE

Kiran A.U.

The land of Kerala has a resplendent tradition of cultural innovations in various spectrum like Dance, Drama, Architecture, Music, Iconography and so on. Among the different aspects of cultural formation Architecture stood in the first position due to its direct intervention to lives of every person. We have a long tradition of architectural literature which exposes the varied aspects of Kerala Architecture. Among these texts, 'Vāstuśāstra' which is considered to be the fourth 'upaveda' gives a comprehensive information regarding the architectural glory of ancient Kerala. The term '*vāstu*' is derived from the root '*vas*' which means to live. There exists a plethora of sources regarding the Architectural peculiarities of Kerala which include *Tantrasamuccaya* of Chennas Narayan Nampoothiri, the *Vāstuvidyā* of Tirumangalathu Nālakanīhanmīsat, *Manuṣyālayacandrikā* and the *Devālayacandrikā* of Thirumangalathu Nīlakanīhan Mīsat, the *Śilparatna* of Śrīkumāran Nampoothiri, the *Prayogamañjari*, the *Mayamata*, the *Śilpaśātra*, etc. are the prominent works in this regard and there are some anonymous works too.

Kerala produced a few manuals in Sanskrit which give a detailed information regarding the architectural pattern of ancient Kerala, which even today stand as authoritive treatises on Architecture. The *Tantrasamuccaya* (1427-28 AD) the

Manuṣyālayacandrikā (between fifteenth and seventeenth centuries *Devālayacandrikā* (fifteenth, seventeenth century), *Śilparatna* (sixteenth centaury) and *Vāstuvidyā* are notable works in this field.

Tantrasamuccaya (fifteenth century AD)

The *Tantrasamuccaya* of Chennas Nārāyaṇan Nampoothiri is a commendable treatise on temple architecture, sculpture and rituals. It is an unquestionable authority on the laws and methods for the construction of a shrine, installation of the idol, daily worship, renovation, reconstruction and allied rituals. The entire work is divided into twelve *paṭalas* consisting of 2896 verses.

A general sketch of the topics in the twelve sections may be given as follows:

1. Details regarding the selection of a Guru, the selection of the site for the construction of the temple, the ceremony of the *Nidhikalaṇa*—a potful of riches, laying of the bricks, the placing of the foundation stone and the selection of suitable granite for the construction.
2. Characteristics of the temple proper called *prāsāda*, its measurements, the details of the construction, the characteristics of the idol and its seat, types of idols and their measurements, *Balipīṭhas*—the oblation stones, and the measurements of the five-fold fortifications.
3. Purification of the site, sowing of the seeds in the site to test its fertility, preparation of the idol, ceremonies connected with the cleaning of the temple, placing of the idol in water and its further purification and related rituals.
4. Purification of the *manṇḍapas,* the temple halls, offerings of oblations to minor deities that guard the inner part of the shrine, the deities that guard the gate-ways, purifications of the spot where the

ceremonies with the *kalasas* or pots filled with sanctified water are place, kindling of the sacred fire, worship of the bed to place the idol horizontally before installing it, and bathing of the idol with sanctified water.

5. The fifth paṭala of the work deals with the installation of the idol. *Adhivāsana homa,* and the rules and regulations connected with *pūjā.*

इति तन्त्रसमुच्चये समाप्ति समवाप्तः पटलोऽत्र पञ्चमोऽभूत्।
निजभावनमन्त्रविम्बपीठाद्याधिवासार्चनतद्धुतादियुक्त।।[1]

6. The sixth paṭala provides a detail information regarding the fixation of the deity, consecration (*abhiṣekha*), *mahābalipāda, nikṣepa,* etc.

इति तन्त्रसमुच्चये रहस्यागमसारः पटलः समाप्ति षष्ठः।
प्रकटीकृतपादपीठपीठप्रतिमावारकपीठिकाप्रतिष्ठः।।[2]

The critic of the *Tantrasamuccaya,* i.e., *Vimarśinī* by Chennas Sankaran Nampoothiri (son of Chennas Narayanan Nampoothiri) provides a deep insight into the work. The author informs that the work had received popularity and acceptance during fifteenth century.

Śeṣasamuccaya

Śeṣasamuccaya was an important work belonging to the Tantra tradition and the author is Kūnuśarma, the deciple of Cennus Nārāyaṇan Nampoothiri. It is the complementary work to the *Tantrasamuccaya.* Cennas Śankaran Nampoothiri, the son and successor of Cennas Nārāyaṇan Nampootiri. In addition to these Kuśikkuttu Maheswarabhattathiri wrote a commentary on the *Śeṣasamuccaya,* i.e. *Śeṣasamuccaya Vyākhyā.* Both the two works have popularity and authenticity among the *Tantris* of Kerala.

Manuṣyālayacandrikā

The *Manusyālayacandrikā* is a unique work dealing exclusively with construction of residential buildings, which was compiled by Tirumangalatu Nīlakanīhan. It is believed that the work was composed during *c.* AD 15th century and it was a dossier connected with the then existing architectural literature and associated knowledge. The text has a pan Indian outlook in which the basic techniques, theories, and philosophy of Indian *Vāstuvidyā* pertaining to residential buildings have been consolidated and it is the most authentic text in this regard even now.

The text is divided into seven chapters. The first chapter starts with the list of texts referred to by the author. It deals with the guilds of craftsmen and duties of each guild. It also gives rules for selection of land. In chapter 2, procedure for fixing the cardinal directions and the major reference lines are detailed. This chapter also contains prescriptions on the zoning rules in deciding the locations of the building. It deals extensively with the concept of '*Vāstupuruṣamaṇḍala*'. The system of measurement used in 'Vāstuvidya' is described in chapter 3. It also deals with the rules for planning settlements. The architectural formula for orientation viz. the *yoni* concept and the astrological factors of *āya, vyāya,* etc. are also included in this chapter.

The chapter 4 deals with the characteristics of different classes of buildings while chapters 5, 6 and 7 describe the details of the different elements of the building. They also give details of location of the different facilities in a house and also of the subsidiary buildings like cattle-shed, entrance-gate, etc. The book is thus a comprehensive treatise on planning, designing and construction of residential buildings.

The Relevance of this work

There are more than a dozen commentaries on the *Manuṣyālayacandrikā* written in Malayalam. This shows the popularity and acceptance of the work as a standard one not only among craftsmen but also among laymen. The style and language of these books are such that they can be followed only by those who have some knowledge of 'Vāstuśāstra'. Moreover, illustrations are very rare in these works. Hence an illustrated engineering commentary which gives emphasis to the technological aspects and which can be easily followed by all becomes important. This will specially enable engineers and architects to understand the philosophy, design theories and practices followed in India so as to enable them to integrate this knowledge with modern developments in engineering and architecture. This will definitely pave way for evolving an Indian style which is relevant and appropriate in today's India.

Devālayacandrikā

It is a work dealt with the construction of temples and idols for worship. Manuscripts of the text are not available in India. In its perfect form and the Malayalam commentary on the same reveals the existence and uniqueness of the work. After the introductory stanza the author mentions the rules for the selection of site for the shrine. The selected site is then measured and consecrated with ritualistic purifications. Then follows the details regarding the actual construction of the temple. The specifications of outer walls, pillars, sanctum sanctorium, drains, doorways, decorations on the walls, roofings, spires, halls, etc. are given. The manuscript ends abruptly with the verse 171, the last subject treated being the idol of Śiva.

Śilparatna

The *Śilparatna* was a *c.* sixteenth century composition dealing with Śilpa by Śrīkumāran Nampoothiri and it is a comprehensive work which is concerned with each and every aspect of Śilpa. The work was composed by the order and patronage of Champakassery Poorīṃamtirunl̦ Thampuram.

The work gives information regarding sacred knowledge like *citralakṣaṇa, vāhalakṣaṇa, dhanurlakṣaṇa,* etc.

The commentaries are also mentionable, especially *Śilparatnambhāṇa* of a Nampoothiri of Thykkattillam. The work is otherwise known as '*Thykkattu bhāṣa*' or *Adukke*: it contains more than six hundred Maṇipravāla ślokas which gained great popularity among the carpenters (*aṣārīs*) of Kerala.

Īśānaśivagurudevapaddhati

The Tantrpadhati also known as *Īśānaśivagurudevapaddhati* named after the author *Īśānaśivagurudeva* is an elaborate treatise dealing with the various aspects of Tantra. The work consists of nearly 18000 stanzas in various metres and divided into a total of 119 paṭalas of varying length. The subjects explained are the construction of temples, consecration of idols, modes of worship, festivals, japa, homa, etc.

The work is divided into four parts namely: 1. Sāmānya-pāda containing paṭalas 1 to 14, 2. Mantrapāda consisting patalas 15 to 52, 3. Kriyāpāda having paṭalas 1 to 64 and 4. Yogapāda dealing with paṭalas 1 to 3. The first 52 paṭalas form the *pūrvārdha* and the next 72 paṭalas form the uttarārdha as designated by the author.

Prayogamañjarī

Among the Tāntrika works produced in Kerala the *Prayogamañjari* often referred to simply as *Mañjarī* is one of the earliest and most important compendiums. Later writers like Īśanaśivaguru and others have heavily drawn materials from it and considered it to be most authoritative. The work is conceived as a manual for the practical use of Namputiri Brahmins who are enjoined to perform rituals in Kerala temples.

The work starts with praising tutelary deity of the author i.e., Śiva. The concluding part reveals the identity of the author as Ravipaṣṇita. The entire work has been divided into

21 paṭalas and the issues discussed are: *ācārya parigraham. bhāparigraham, vāstuyogam, nārtakādhānam, garbhādhānam, prāsādalakṣaṇam, śilālakṣaṇam, liṅgalakṣaṇa, dīkṣā, aṅguram* (pinnacla), *jalādhivāsana, rakṣākhaṇavāstu, liṅgasuddhi, adhivāsana, pratiṣṭhā, arcanā, caturdhā, divasasnapana, utsavam* and so on and so forth.

The *Prayogamañjarī* explains almost each and every aspect of temple architecture and worship. The work is not dedicated to any god or goddess. It has got widespread momentum due to the perpetual usage by the Tantrics. During fifteenth century Trivikraman wrote a commentary named '*Pradyota*' to *Prayogamañjarī.*

Mayamata

The *Mayamata* attributed to Maya, the celestial architect was popular in Kerala and formed a source book for architecture for many Kerala writers like *Nīlakaṇṭha,* the author of *Manuṣyālayacandrikā.* Ullur unequivocally stated that *Mayamata* was a Malayalam work. Albeit Nīlakaṇṭhan mentions two Mayamatas but only one is found. The entire work is divided into 34 chapters, but scholars have the view that in addition to these 34 there may be four chapters more.

Conclusion

In brief, the researcher would like to mention some important findings and aspects regarding the Architecture of Kerala. It is a generally acceptable fact that the Malayalam works on architecture had their roots in the Sanskrit texts. The architectural styles like Nālukettu, Ettukettu, Pathinṛukettu, Kīhambalam, Chuttambalam, Śrīkovil, etc. are based on these authentic texts. Similarly, the *darśana* (facade), foundation, position of the house (*sthāna*) etc. are determined by the rules and measures mentioned in these texts. Among these texts *Manuṣyālayacandrikā* has been widely used as an authentic work for the construction of residential buildings. It is an interesting fact that modern engineers are using our traditional works on Architecture for the construction and decoration of modern buildings. The structure laid in our ancient manuals are still followed in the modern construction purposes.

References

1. Nārāyaṇa, *Tantrasamuccaya,* Paṭala. 5, p. 250.
2. Ibid., Paṭala. 6, verses 141, p. 293.
3. Ed. T. Ganapati Sastri, Trivandrum Sanskrit Series nos. 69, 72, 77 and 83. Trivandrum, 1920, 1921, 1922 and 1925 (in 4 vols.). Reprinted with a general introduction by Dr. N.P. Unni, Delhi, 1987 (in 4 vols.)
4. Transcript No. 20 of Trivandrum Manuscripts Library.
5. K.V. Sarma, The Devālayacandrikā,*Adayar Library Bulletin 25,* 1961, pp. 582–86.

18

GLIMPSES OF KERALA ARCHITECTURE IN MANIPRAVALA WORKS

NADUVATTOM GOPALAKRISHNAN

Building construction with plan and sketch seems to have come into existence in Kerala round about the dawn of the 9th century CE. The earliest historical record related to the construction of a temple in Kerala goes back to 823 AD in which year the famous Śiva temple at Kandiyur near Mavelikara was consecrated. From there onwards we get several references in inscriptions regarding the construction and consecration of temples. Regarding palaces and dwelling houses also there are references in old documents and early literary works, for instance Panaṅkāvil, Karippukkalam, Tṛppāppūr palaces and Vīramāṇikyam, Veḷḷuur, Kuṟuṅṅāt, Kurumuḷikkal houses.

We get evidences of indigenous tradition of the architecture of ancient Kerala from the descriptions seen in the *Uṇṇunīlisandeśam,* a messenger poem of fourteenth century CE on Śri Padmanābhasvāmī Temple at Thiruvananthapuram and Vīramāṇikyam the dwelling house of the heroine Uṇṇunīli at Kaduturutti. The earliest temples, houses and palaces were built of wood and bricks. Kerala architecture comprises temples and dwelling houses which were built of mud, wood and stone. The tradition is that houses of wood and stone were built only for kings and gods. Those who were out of *cāturvarṇya* (four caste system) had to live in mud houses. Dwelling houses are found as adaptations of palaces in four or eight wings, *Nālukettu* or *Eṭṭukeṭṭu.*

Śrī Padmanābhaswāmi temple

Regarding the temple structure no description is seen in the *Uṇṇunīlisandeśam.* The order given to the worship of the Gods installed in Śrī Padmanābhasvāmī Temple enables one to reconstruct the internal structure of that temple. The poet asks the messenger first to worship the chief deity Padmanābha and there after Lord Narasiṃha, Vedavyāsa, Viṣvksēna, Rāma, Lakṣmaṇa and Hanumān. After that the poet directs the messenger to proceed to the *Maṇḍapa* where Garuḍa is installed. Near the southern side of the *Maṇḍapa* the idol of Śrīkṛṣṇa is seen lying in a cradle. The poet asks the messenger to give salutation to that deity. There after the messenger entered the outer pathway to worship the lord Ayyappa installed in the shrine at the south-west corner. After worshipping the Ayyappa the messenger proceeded to the shrine of Tiruvāmpāṭikṛṣṇa situated in the north-west direction, which seems to be the oldest one in the Śrī Padmanābha Temple complex. Then the messenger proceeds to the shrine of Kṣetrapāla situated on the north side of the pathway and moves to the eastern side where the Valiya Balikkallu is situated and finally gaves his obeyance to Śrī Padmanābha and went out of the temple through western gate.

The internal structure of Śri Padmanābhasvāmī Temple at the time of the *Uṇṇunilisandēśam* (*c.* 1350-1390 CE) can be reconstructed based on the description mentioned above.

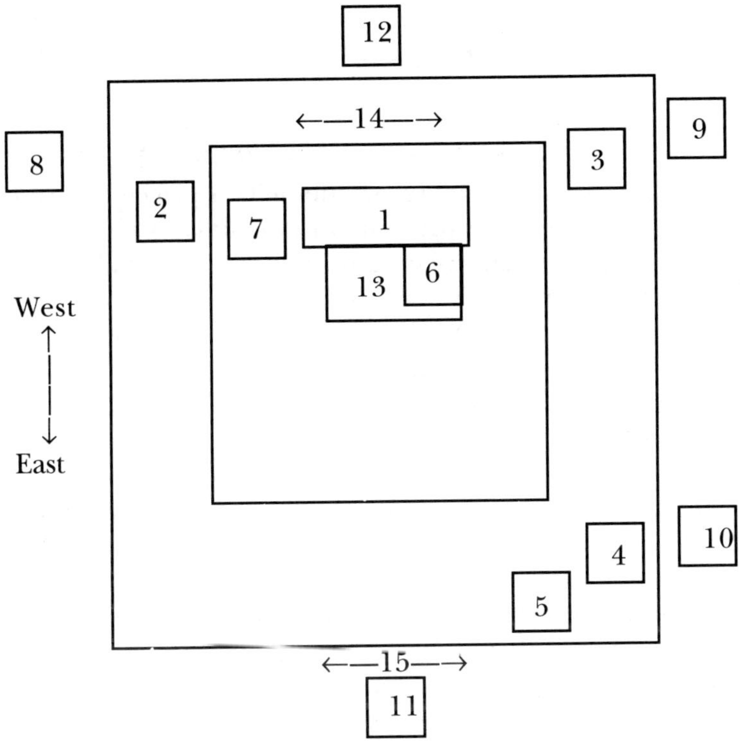

1. Anantaśayanam (verse 37, 38, 39, 40, 41)
2. Narasiṃhamūrtti shrine (verse 42)
3. Vēdavyāsa shrine (verse 43)
4. Viṣvksēna shrine (verse 44)
5. Rāma, Lakṣmaṇa and Hanumān chamber (verse 44)
6. Garuḍa idols (verse 44)
7. Uṇṇikṛṣṇa lying in a cradle (verse 45)
8. Ayyappa shrine (verse 45)
9. Tiruvāmpāṭi Kṛṣṇa shrine (verse 46, 47)
10. Kṣētrapāla (the deity guarding the temple) (verse 48)
11. Valiya Balipīṭham (altar for performing sacrifice) (verse 49)
12. Western gate
13. Maṇḍapa (erected hall)

14. Dīpāśālā (light chamber)
15. Nālampalam (the structure surrounding the sanctum sanctorium)

The Śrīkōvil was in square shape. Within there is the *Garbhagṛha* where the image of the deity is placed. In front of the *Garbhagṛha* (sanctum sanctorium) is situated a maṇḍapa on a square plan and built with pyramidal roof. Surrounding this there was a corridor known as *Dīpaśālā*. The entrance to the Nālampalam is through the eastern portion where the Balipīṭham is situated.

Uṇṇunīli's Nālukeṭṭu

The house of Uṇṇunīli consisted of four rooms joined together in a rectangular form with a yard in the centre inside. These structures are called *Nālukeṭṭu* though that word is not attested in the messenger poem. The basement and foundation of this house seems to be built of laterite and the other portions such as the columns, caves, the gables, the overhanging roof were built of timber. This house faces the east. The entrance is constructed at quite a little distance which consists of a door in the centre and beautiful pathway. The anonymous poet also gives the scale of each wing (*keṭṭu*) which is found in strict conformity with the principle of Vāstuśāstra.

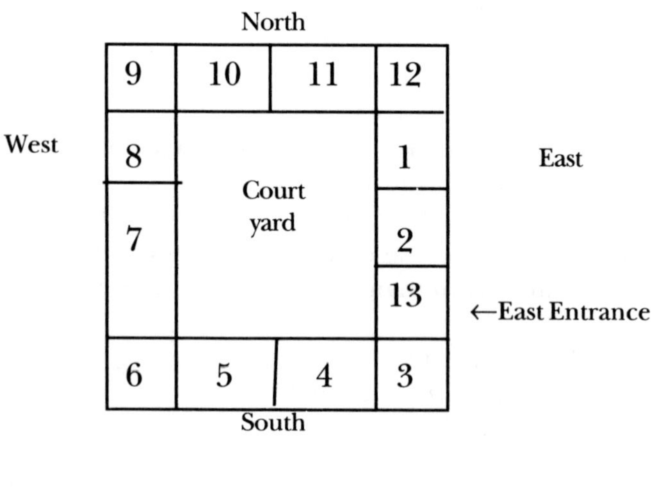

1 2, 3 13	Kiḷakkinni-east wing	40 kōl 16 aṅgulam circumfeerence
4, 5 6	Tekkini-south wing	38 kōl 8 aṅgulam
7 8 9	Paṭiññāṟṟini-west wing	39 kōl 16 aṅgulam
10 11 12	Vaṭakkini-north wing	39 kōl 16 aṅgulam

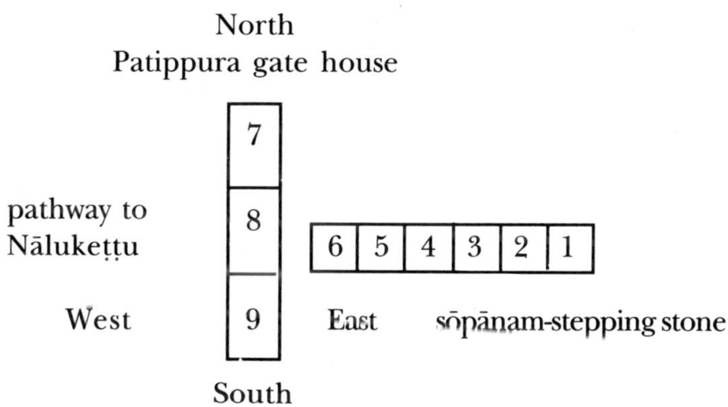

1, 2, 3, 4, 5, 6-sōpānam-stepping stone to go up
height of the stepping stone—5 aṅgulam
width 3 cāṇ (27 inches)
7, 8, 9 Paṭippura gate house with apartments
length 6 k ōl[1]
8 door width 1 kōl 14 aṅgulam

The unknown author of the *Uṇṇunīlisandēśam,* well versed in architecture, also gives the measurements of the Nālukeṭṭu of *Uṇṇunīli* in verse number 35, 36 of the second part of the poem. In verses number 33 and 34 he gives the measurements of the pathway and the front gate with apartment. It really creates surprise when we see the skill of the poet in narrating the scale and measurements of a house in an attractive poetic rhythm. The half of the *Tekkini* of the *Nālukeṭṭu* was used as bed room and the remaining portion for receiving the relatives. *Kiḷakkini* was intended for accommodating the guests. Paṭiññaṟṟini was used for keeping valuable goods and Vaṭakkini for cooking and related family affairs. The house description found in the *Uṇṇunīlisandēśam* is a clear proof to the architectural skill of the carpenters of Kerala in the construction field by taking into consideration the climate and building materials available.

Trees like Jack tree are best planted in the compound around the house. The distance between each of them must be double that of their height when they attain maximum growth. Coconut trees and areacanut trees are to be grown on the outer side of the compound, thus Uṇṇunīli's house presented a fine picture with a large compound. Almost all agricultural products like coconuts, vegetables, medicinal herbs, etc. were available around the house. There was one pond and one well in the compound (verse 37, 41).

References

1. 1 aṅgulam -1¼ inch
   28,- kōl.
   1 cāṇ - 9 inches
   The kōls are of different measurement and show changes according to latitude. Generally the length of kōl at Kerala is calculated as 28 inches.

19

CLASSICAL KERALA ARCHITECTURE AND THE NOVEL STRUCTURE OF C.V. RAMANPILLAI WITH SPECIAL REFERENCE TO THE MĀRTAṆḌAVARMĀ

S.S. SREEKUMAR

The *mārgī* (classical) tradition of Kerala architecture is documented in the palm leaf manuscripts obtained from several places in the State. It clearly indicates the influence of Indian classical tradition in which the concept of *Nalukettu* is the actual form of Kerala architecture. As *Koodiyattam* is said to be the unique theatrical form of Sanskrit drama, *Nalukettu* is said to be the Kerala form of Indian classical architecture. Kerala model of classical architecture like *Nalukettu, Ettukettu, Pathinaarukettu* functioned in the society as a particular weapon to maintain the hierarchy of the society. There is particular function in each part of the *Nalukettu*. The entry of other people into the house is restricted. The four portions of the structure, *Vadakkini* (northern portion), *Thekkini* (southern portion), *Kizhakkini* (eastern portion) and *Padinjatti* (western portion) are meant for different purposes as for worship, bed, cook, dine and store. The verandah going through the four portions inside the structure allow all the inhabitants to mix with one another. The external verandahs of each four portions are meant to entertain different people like the noblemen in the front and the servants, washerwomen, barbers and the tenants in the side and back portions of a *Nalukettu*.There will be a *Nadumuttam* (quadrangle) in the midst of the structure. There will also be a *Padippura* (gatehouse) in front of the structure which enables the inhabitants to restrict the entry of the then backward classes (Bhaskaranunni: 1984). Only the elite classes of the society like Namboothiris, members of royal families and lords possessed the right to build such structures and they alone could afford to build such grand structures. If we closely examine these structures we can notice that such a tradition existed by eliminating majority of the people of the society like the then backward classes.

In deep contrast with this classical tradition of architecture, there also existed a *Deśī* (folk) tradition. The simplest form of it is a rectangular base and a coniferous roof. This is the wide accepted model throughout the state/ country by the poor, marginal classes of the society. This is also the form of architecture adopted by the working class of the Kerala society through centuries. It is interesting to note that this form is also adopted for the structure of primitive worship places like *Nada, Mandakam* and *Kottam* of Southern Travancore, South Malabar and North Malabar regions respectively. In the famous poem *Poothappattu,* Edassery mentions *"Parayante mandakam kandaanunni"* (Unni saw the *Mandakam* of *Paraya).* In another poem *Duravasthā,* Kumaran Aasan clearly indicates that the little hut of *Chaathan* is 'like a mushroom in the boundary of the field'. 'That is not circular, conical or rectangular and there was not a glance of the technique of an architect', Aasan comments.

Architecture of the *Manuṣyalāyas* (the habitat of human beings) is not only a mixture of building materials or the calculation of structures, it obviously reflects the mindset of its inhabitants, their material practices, cultural needs and their world view. This world view is only found to be seen in literature, which is the expression of the human soul as a whole.

Though Malayalam literature has a short history of eight hundred years, it reflects the concept of architecture in both classical and folk traditions. One of our master narrators,

C.V. Raman Pillai in the first novel of his historical trilogy on Travancore portrays the classical Kerala architecture. His silence on the life of the marginal classes as well as their living places is to be noted well. This paper intends to study how the concept of classical architecture shaped his literary content, plot and also the narrative style.

We already noted that the poets like Kumaran Aasan and Edassery Govindan Nair mentioned the existence of the *Deśī sampradāya* (folk tradition) of Kerala architecture in their works. In C.V. Raman Pallai's *Martandavarmā,* we can not only notice that it reflects the classical architecture of Kerala but also the determining factors which shaped the structure of the novel.

Space and Time in the Novel

Space and Time are the major components which determine the structure of novel. The characters in a novel are developed through the time in a given space. The continuity of incidents taking place in the given space evolving through the time gives a structure to the novel. One of our master narrators C.V. Raman Pillai influenced by the historical romance of Sir Walter Scott— *'Ivanho',* chose the new genre named novel for his aesthetic practice. While Chandumenon, another novelist of the same period portrays the contemporary society in his novels *Indulekhā* and *Śāradā,* the social novels of simple structure, C.V. Raman Pillai wrote about the past society in a sophisticated and stylized structure depicting exaggerated characters in a historical background.

The concept of Vāstumaṇḍala

In classical architecture there exists a concept of *Vāstu-maṇḍala.* The earth in which we live is treated as the biggest *Vāstumaṇḍalā* (Architectural plane) and the continents, nations, states and the piece of land where we build houses are microforms of this *Vāstumaṇḍala* which are also treated as *Vāstumaṇḍalas* (Kanippayyor: 2000). In this sense the princely state of Travancore is the basic *Vāsthumaṇḍala* of his historical trilogy along with *Martandavarma*. In this novel, Padmanabhapuram palace, Charotte palace, Kalliyan-kadu, Chempakasseri tharavadu, the house of Kudamon Pillai and the house of Mankoikkal Kurup are the different architectural planes where the characters of C.V. Raman Pillai lived their lives.

Along with the trilogy, the *Martandavarmā* shares some particular characteristics. The characters of these novels are historical characters in a fictitious mould. They are not life-like human beings. Not only his characters but also his plot, diction and background are complicated in nature. His criticism about the social circumstances came into being through his novels. A direct reading of his novels gives an impression that he tries to glorify the Dynasty of Travancore. The names of the novels were undoubtedly of the rulers of Travancore; Anizham Thirunal Marthandavarmā and Rāmavarma. But they are not the central characters of the novel. Ananta-padmanābhan and Subhadrā are the leading characters of the novel that controls the story line of the respective novels. The complexity is the outcome of the complex life portrayed in his novels. The factors which made the novel *Martandavarmā* a historical romance are the usage of complex Sanskrit influenced sentences, the way of expression which usually Kathakali follows and sure enough the descriptions of ancient and traditional architectural grandeur of Kerala especially of the aristocratic households like *Nalukettu, Ettukettu,* etc. In the *Martandavarmā,* Ettuveettil Pillais, Ugraharipanchananan, Perinchakkottu Kunchu-mayitti Pillai and Kaaliyudayan Chandrakkaran; though they played negative roles in the trilogy, they are at the heights of the novel. As K.C. Narayanan pointed out in his beautiful essay *Malayalikalude Ratrikal* (The nights of Malayalis), the importance given to the negative characters is a particular peculiarity of Kerala's own theatre Kathakali. When the roles of gods and kings are enacted by minor artists the negative roles are usually given to master artists like Kalamandalam Ramankutty Nair and Late Champakkulam Pachu Pillai and Vellinezhi Nanu Nair etc.

The art of Kathakali influenced C.V. Raman Pillai a lot. In his novel as Dr. K. Bhaskaran Nair observes, C.V. Raman Pillai used the *Bhāvaprakāśana sampradāya'* of Kathakali. It tried to *'rasoddīpana'* with' *bṛhatkaraṇa'*. That means C.V. Raman Pillai used the style of expansion to generate the feelings of the readers. He incorporates literary allusions from not only the Itihāsapurāṇas, but also from Kerala literature and the literature of performing arts, including Kathakali. The Marthandavarmā is also an example of this rule.

Kathakali and Nalukettu—C.V's alienation techniques

C.V. Raman Pillai wanted to estrange his characters from the petty present. He equates his characters with the characters of the Purāṇas. He uses similes and metaphors from the classical literature. Chandrakkaran began to walk and became *"Chandrakkaran dasakandharan paadaradhathe aarohanam cheythu" (Chandrakkaran* who was Rāvaṇa ascended the chariot of his feet). Russian formalist Victor Shklovsky states that the main technique in literature is unfamiliarisation. C.V. Raman Pillai through his grand style alienates the common man from his novels. It intends that the readers of the novel must be the noble men of the society of higher caste Hindus. In his novels there are only characters from the elite classes like Kings, lords, Brahmins and Nairs. The then depressed classes like *Channan, Maravar* and *Parayar* also enters the structure of the novel but they usually play minor roles in the novel.

In Kathakali no character can speak. It is an art form of silence. This technique is used for the alienation of the characters from the present. There are also other techniques like through *mudrās* and the peculiar *āhāryābhinaya* with the characters of *triguṇa* i.e. *Pacha, Kathi, Kari, Thaadi, Minukku* representing the *sattva, rajas,* and *tamas guṇas.* The semicircular crowns and the *Chutti* through particular colours especially green, black and red make the characters alien from the present. The huge *Uduthukett,* the grand skirt made up of pillows and sacs are also used for this purpose. Through these estrangement techniques the characters of Kathakali estrange themselves from the petty men and the women of the present. So majority of the marginalized people also alienate themselves from Kathakali, the classical art form. For their aesthetic appreciation they make their own folk art forms both related to culture and art. *Theyyam, Padayani, Mudiyeettu* are examples for the first and *Porattu, Kakkarissi* are for the rest.

The *Martandavarmā* obviously shows the description of architectural grandeur which makes the structure of the novel to alienate from the petty present. The narration of the Chempakasseri house which spread over two pages in the novel pictures the architectural glory of the past. This *Vāstuśilpamaṇḍala* surprises the ordinary reader and it brings the awareness of the glorified past.

In this *arappura* (bedroom) the main incidents of the novel takes place. This is the bedroom of Parvathyamma, the lover of Anantapadmanābhan, who is the heroine of the novel. *Nalukettu,* the native form of classical architecture is meant for the restricted entry of the depressed classes says P. Bhaskaranunni (Bhaskaranunni: 1984) in his book *Kerala in the ninteenth century*. In the *Mārtandavarmā* the *Karanavar* of the family cannot enter that room. As a Brahmin, Sundarayyan easily enters the room and tries to influence Karthyayaniamma, mother of Parvathyamma to persuade her to marry Sree Padmanabhan Thampi. Sanku Aasan who is the watchman of the armoury tries to question the entry of Sundarayya and he is prevented entry to the Northern block. One day Sree Padmanabhan Thampi stays at *Chempakassery* and try to molest the girl. With the help of Sanku, Aasan Ananthapadmanabhan enters this room and prevents him from the act.

The description of the architecture not only alienates the ordinary reader but also takes part in the mysterious incidents which determine the formal structure of the novel. This classical concept of architecture became the central nucleus of the art of the novel of C.V. Raman Pillai, '*Martandavarmā*.

Bibliography

1. Bhaskaranunni, P. *Pathompathaam Noottaandile Keralam,* Kerala Sahithya Academy, Thrissur, 1984, p. 48.
2. Kanippayyor, in Mohanākshan Nair, ed., *Vasthujnana-parvam,* M.G. University, Kottayam, 2000, p. 18.
3. Narayanan, K.C. *Majayaliyude Rathrikal,* D.C. Books, Kottayam, 2004, p. 111.

20

MANUSCRIPTS RELATED TO ARCHITECTURE IN GOVERNMENT ORIENTAL MANUSCRIPTS LIBRARY, CHENNAI

J.M. Gandhimathi

The Government Oriental Manuscript Library and Research Centre (GOML and RC) Chennai is a unit under the State Department of Archaeology. It is a veritable treasure-house of ancient knowledge housing 50,180 palm-leaf manuscripts, 22,134 paper manuscripts and 26,556 rare printed books. Started in 1869, this library is the repository of rare manuscripts and books in various languages such as Tamil, Sanskrit, Telugu, Kannada, Marathi, Pali, Urdu, Arabic, Persian, Sinhalese, etc. covering subjects such as Mathematics, Astronomy, Siddha, Ayurveda, Unani, Veda, Āgama, Architecture, Music, Sculpture, Fine arts, History, Grammar, Literature and many others. Scholars from all over India and abroad visit the GOML to access these rare manuscripts and books. It is an excellent resource centre for doing research leading to Ph.D. The collections of Colonel Mackenzie(1754-1821), Dr. Leyden and Mr. C.P. Brown constitute the nucleus of the vast collection of manuscripts preserved in the Government Oriental Manuscripts Library, Madras, which consists of manuscripts of works in Literature, History, Philosophy and Science, written in South Indian and other Oriental Languages, and of Kaifiyats and inscriptions found in many places belonging to different periods. This paper gives a comprehensive account of manuscripts related to Architecture in GOML, which would kindle the interest of scholars and students who wish to pursue their research in the field of Architecture based on manuscripts.

1. *Aṃsumadbheda: Kāśyapīya No. 1302*

Paper manuscript; size 13.25 × 8 inches, pages 522, lines 21 on a page; character. Grantha; Complete-1083 Paṭalas. A treatise laying down rules for the construction of dwelling houses, palaces, temples, storied mansions, etc. and of windows, doors, porches, gateways, towers connected therewith and for the making of images of gods especially of the various manifestations of God Śiva. The work is attributed to Kāśyapa who is said to have learnt this science from God Śiva. It deals with 86 subjects including: *Gopuralakṣaṇam, Vinayakalakṣaṇam, Parivāravidhi, Nāsikalakṣaṇam, Nagarādhividhī, Toraṇalakṣaṇam, Manopāgāram, Maṇḍapalakṣaṇam, Prākāralakṣaṇam, Sukāsanam, Kalyāṇasundaralakṣaṇam, Ārdhanārīśvaralakṣaṇam, Gajamūrtilakṣaṇam, Pāṣupatamūrtilakṣaṇam, Dakṣiṇāmūrtilakṣaṇam* etc. Copying is said to have been finished on Friday, the 30th day of the month of Citrai in the year Taraṇa.

2. *Aṃśumadbheda: with Tamil meaning No 13033*

Palm-leaf manuscript-size 27×2 inches; pages 126; lines 9 on a page: character Kanarese. Begins on folio 47a. The other works herein are the *Mānasāra* (with Telugu notes) 39a, *Mayamatavāstuśāstra* 1a. Breaks off in the 59th adhāya same as the above work and with meaning in Tamil.

3. *Mayamatavāstuśāstram with Tamil meaning No 13034*

Paper: size-13×8 inches; pages 390-22; lines per page; chapter Grantha and Tamil. Begins on folio 1a. The other works herein is *Śilpaśāstra* 196a. Contains adhyāyas 1 to 36, 13 to 18, 24 and 23 with Tamil meaning. Rules for laying out and the planning of towns is given here and the work is attributed to sage Maya

4. *Mayamatavāstuśāstram with Telugu meaning No 13035*
Pages 74 and 9 lines per page. Contains 1 to 32 adhyāyas; complete. Same work as above with Telugu meaning.

5. *Mayamatavāstuśāstram No 13036*
Paper: size 12.5×9.5 inches-pages 5, 22 lines per page. Begins with folio 170a. Contains some portions towards the end of the third adhyāya as well as description of *Sphaṭikaliṅga.*

6. *Mayamatavāstuśāstram No 13037*
Paper: size 11×8.5 inches; pages 6; 18 lines per page; character Telugu. Begins on folio 21380 the other work herein is *Mānasāra* 180 contains the third adhyāya complete and the 34th incomplete; but wants the beginning in the 33rd adhyāya. Same work as the above.

7. *Mayamatavāstuśāstram with Telugu meaning No 13038*
Palm-leaf; size 14.5×1.25 inches; pages 94; 5 lines per page; chapter Telugu. Contains 12 adhyāyas complete; wants beginning in the first adhyāya. This work gives rules for the making of images, temples, etc. It is attributed to Maya. It is followed by meaning in Telugu by Gannanacharya.

8. *Mayamataśilpaśāstram with Telugu Tika No 13039*
Palm-leaf; size-14.35×I.5 inches; pages 36; 5 lines per folio, character Telugu. Same as above work but breaks off in the fourth adhyāya.

9. *Mānavavāstulakṣaṇam No 13040*
Paper; size 8.75 × 5.5 inches; 5 pages; 8 lines per page, character Devanagari. Begins on folio 19a. The other work herein is *Santānadīpikā.* Contains 9 stanzas only which deals with the selection of site and the surveying and plotting of a ground apparently for building purposes.

10. *Mānasāra No 13041*

Paper; size 13.25×8 inches; pages 495; 18 lines per page, character Grantha. Contains adhyāyas 1 to 72; complete. An extensive treatise dealing with surveying and plotting of land for building purposes, with the planning of villages and towns, with the construction of houses and temples together with the ceremonial rites to be observed on such occasions and with the making of images of different deities, etc. The headings of the adhyāyas specially the first adhyāya indicate elaborately the subjects dealt within them.

11. *Mānasāra No 13042*

Pages 330; lines 22 on a page. Same work as above. Begins in the course of the seventeenth adhyāya and contains to the end of the work. The names, the numbering and the arrangement of the adhyāyas as found in this manuscript are different from those found in the manuscript descibed under the previous number.

12. *Mānasāra No 13043*

Pages 20; lines 6 on a page; Begins on folio 26a and contains the adhyāyas 37 to 40 but with the beginning in the thirty-seventh adhyāya and the end in the fortieth Adhyāya.

13. *Mānasāra No 13044*

Pages 18; lines 9 on a page; contains the thirty-fourth adhyāya which lacks the beginning portion and the thinty-ninth adhyāya. Same work as above with Telugu meaning.

14. *Mānasāra No 13045*

Pages 411; 18 lines on a page. Begins on folio 1a, incomplete. Same work as above

15. *Śilpaśāstram: Agastyam No 13046*

Pages 9; 15 lines on a page. The portion contained in this

manuscript deals with the astrological points so far as they are considered pertinent to Architecture.

16. *Śilpaśāstram: Agastyam No 13047*

Palm-leaf; size 10.75×l inches; pages 24; lines 4 on a page; character Grantha. Same work as above and treats of *āyādilakṣaṇam*

17 *Śilpaśāstram No 13048*

Pages 192; lines 22 on a page. A work on *Śilpaśāstra* containing details of the measurement etc. in connection with the making of the images especially if the various forms of Lord Śiva. The work is compiled from three works, viz. *Aṃśumadbheda, Viśvakarmīya* and *Agastīyaśilpa*

18. *Śilpaśāstram No 13049*

Paper; size 9.5×7.5 inches; pages 218; lines 21 on a page; character Telugu. Same work as above.

19. *Śilpaśāstram with Tamil notes No 13050*

Palm-leaf; size 14.5×1.25 inches; pages 132; lines 5 on a page; character Grantha and Tamil. A compilation from three original treatises on Śilpaśāstra.The portion taken from the *Viśvakarmīyaśilpa* deals with certain astrological aspects conducive to gain or loss to the person who begins the laying out of villages or the construction of a building etc. And the portion taken from the *Agastīyaśilpa* deals with the measurement of proportions in images and that taken from the *Mayamataśilpa* deals with the fixing of the various quarters and the laying of a plot of ground for building purposes.

20. *Śilpaśāstram with Tamil meaning No 13051*

Pages 44, lines 22 on a page same work as above

21. *Śilpaśāstram with Tamil meaning No 13052*

Paper; size 6.25×9.25 inches; pages 232; lines 21 on a page, character Devanagari. Contains description of certain divine images and the mode of construction of shrines, temple towers etc.

22. *Śilpaśāstram with Tamil meaning No 13053*
Paper; size 11.75×8 inches; pages 153; lines 26 on a page; character Telugu- incomplete. same work as above.

23. *Śilpaśāstram No 13054*
Palm-leaf; size 10.75×1.25 inches pages; 64 lines; 6 per page; character Telugu; similar to the work above

24. *Śilpaśāstram No 13055*
Pages 26; lines 26 per page. Same work as above. Contains *Berapramāṇalakṣaṇa,* incomplete. Said to have been copied from the manuscript belonging to a Kamsala of Rajahmundry.

25. *Śilpaśāstram No 13056*
Palm-leaf; size 15.75×I.50 inches; pages 109; lines 5 per page; character Grantha. Incomplete and much damaged. Contains treatise on *Madhuchiṣṭalakṣaṇam.*

26. *Śilpaśāstram (Viśvakarmīyam) with Telugu meaning. No 13057*
Palm-leaf; size 11×1.5 inches-pages 100; lines 6 per page; character Telugu. Deals with the construction of houses. The good and evil arising by commencing the construction in certain months are given in the opening stanzas. Name of the scribe Nitla Surappa. Date of copying Saturday the 5th day of the bright fortnight of the Asvija month in the year Jaya.

27. *Śilpasaṅgrahaḥ with Telugu meaning No 13058*
Paper; size, 13.25×8 inches; pages 429; lines 25 per page; character Grantha. A compilation ftom various works on *Śilpa* giving detailed rules for the construction of temples and for

making of images for worship.

28. *Śilpasāraḥ No 13059*

Pages 76; lines 22 on a page. Incomplete. This work contains a series of *Dhyānaślokas* extracted ftom the Purāṇas etc. and they give a description of the several manifestations of various deities of the Hindu pantheon. The description is intended to guide the artist in the making of the images to be used for worship in temples etc.

29. *Sanatkumāravāstuśāstram with Telugu meaning. No 13060*

Pages 45; lines 22 per page. A treatise dealing with the construction of houses and the astrological and ceremonial rites connected with it. The work is attributed to Sanatkumāra who says that he has taken the essence of what is found in the works of Brahman, Indra, Yama, Bhārgava, Aṅgīrasa, Gautama, Gārgya, Manu, Bhṛgu, Viśvakarmā. etc.

30. *Sanatkumāravāstuśāstram No 13061*

Paper; size 11.25×7 inches; pages 29; lines 17 per page, character Devanagari. Begins on folio 317b the other works herein are *Sanandopākhyanamu, Surabhandesvaramu, Caturrvedasaramu, Panditaradhyacarita, Śiva Purāṇasucika.* Incomplete.

31. *Sanatkumāravāstuśāstram with Telugu meaning. No 13062*

Palm-leaf; size I2.75×1.5 inches; pages 48; lines 7 per page; character Telugu; incomplete. Slightly different from above.

32. *Sanatkumāravāstuśāstram with Telugu meaning. No 13063*

Paper; size 12.25×7.75 inches; pages 27; lines 25 per page; character Telugu. Begins on folio 37b. The other works herein are *Niranjanasatakamu, Dattatreyasatakamu, Sadanandayagisatakamu, Yogataravali, Saivastutipadyamulu, Artaraksamanyastkamu* etc. incomplete.

33. *Sanatkumāravāstuśāstram with Telugu meaning. No 13064*
Pages 54; lines 27 per page; similar to the above and incomplete.

34. *Sanatkumāravāstuśāstram with Telugu meaning. No 13064*
Palm-leaf; size 17×1.5 inches; pages 60; lines 5 per page; character Telugu. Similar to the above and incomplete.

35. *Sanatkumāravāstuśāstram with Telugu meaning. No 13065*
Palm-leaf; size 15.75 × 1.5 inches; pages 21; lines 7 per page; character Telugu. Begins on folio 55a. The other works herein are *Jyotiṣa (Muhurtādiviṣaya), Varṣagaṇita* and *Jyotiṣaviṣaya.*

36. *Sanatkumāravāstuśāstram with Kannada meaning. No 13067*
Paper; size 8.5 × 4 inches; pages 87; lines 11 per page; character Kannada. Same as above but with Kannada meaning.

37. *Sanatkumāravāstuśāstram with Telugu meaning. No 13068*
Pages 55; lines 22 per page; Similar to the above and incomplete.

38. *Aṅgulādimānanirṇayaḥ No R-91l(b)*
Palm-leaf. Deals with a kind of measurement having an '*aṅgula*' as its standard used in connection with construction of sacrificial altars.

39. *Adhiṣṭhānalakṣaṇam with Telugu meaning (Śribhāṣya Śrīnivāsācārya) No D-14303*
Pages 20; lines 6 per page; character Telugu. Incomplete. A treatise on Śilpaśāstra dealing with construction of temples.

40. *Vāstupadanyāsavidhiḥ with Malayalam meaning. No-D-8771*
Palm-leaf; 89 folios with 5 lines on a page; incomplete. Deals with the laying out of a temple for the Jina image.

Similar work describing the same rules can be found in Manuscript No-8772

41. *Vāstuvidyā with Malayalam meaning. No-R3385*
Paper; character Devanagari and Malayalam. Complete.

42. *Vāstuśāstravidhānam No-D13592*
Palm-leaf; pages 36; lines 6 per page; size 13.5×I2 inches, character Telugu. Complete, begins on folio 90a. The other works herein are *Salarāmalakshana(Telugu), Jyotiṣaviṣaya, Adhiṣṭhānalakṣaṇa (with* Telugu *meaning), Bṛhajjātaka(with* teiugu meaning) contains 31 adhyāya which treats the proper time for construction of buildings, for the laying down of villages, etc. Name of the scribe-Peddaguruvayya, son of Peddaraja of Velluri family, Karnam of Kottapalayam. Date of completion: Wednesday third day of the bright fortnight in the month of Śrāvaṇa of the year Vikarin.

21

समराङ्गणसूत्रधारे शिलान्यासविधिः

कृष्णकुमार. पी.

प्राचीनभारते बहवः पण्डिताः वास्तुशास्त्रे ख्यातिमलमन्त। तदानीन्तनकालादेव वास्तुशास्त्रस्य नितरां प्राधान्यमसीत्। किन्तु भारतीयवास्तुशास्त्रस्य सर्वत्र सर्वकाले समानरीतिः नासीत्। आलयानां रूपकल्पनासु वैविध्यं दृष्टम्। एकादशशताब्दे विरचिते समराङ्गणसूत्रधारे, तद्वत् अन्यासु कृतिषु च भारतखण्डस्य कालावस्थाम् अनुसृत्य त्रयो विभागाः सन्ति। जांगलम्, अनूपम्, साधारणम् इति।

पुरातनभारते आयुर्वेदः, योगः ज्योतिषम्, वास्तुशास्त्रम्–इति चत्वारि शास्त्राणि प्रधानतया प्रचलितानि आसन्। एतेषां विकासः मनुष्याणां तत्तत्कालोचितम् आवश्यमनुसमभूत्। मानवोपयोगाय वस्तूनां रूपकल्पनां, निर्मितिं च पुरस्कृत्य प्रवृत्तं वेदशास्त्रमेव वास्तुविद्या। प्रपञ्चनियमानुसारेण रूपीकृतस्य वस्तुनः प्रपञ्चस्य च तादात्म्यतत्वमेव वास्तुविद्यायाः मूलम्। प्रपञ्चस्य आलयस्य च उभयोः बन्धः सन्तुलितावस्थाया कर्त्तव्यः। तथा तदालयवासिनाम् आरोग्यम् सम्पत्, सन्तोषः च वर्धयेत इत्येव वास्तुविद्यया उद्दिश्यते।

वास्तु इति पदं विविधप्रकारेण निर्वदन्ति पण्डिताः। ऋग्वेदमनुसृत्य 'वास्तु' इत्यस्य स्थलो वा आलयो वा अथवा उभयौ वा अर्थः। पुराणेषु वास्तु इति पदस्य 'वसन्ति प्राणिनः यत्र' इति अर्थः उक्तः। सर्वप्राणिनां सर्वजीवानां च सन्तुलितया वसनम् एव वास्तुः इति। मृतो वा जीवो वा जीविनाम् आवासकेन्द्रं वास्तुः इति मयमतम्।

वास्तुशास्त्रनमुसृत्य ब्रह्माण्डे वा तस्य सूक्ष्मरूपस्य पिण्डाण्डे वा व्यापृत आत्मा एव वास्तुपुरुषः। वेदान्तमते सर्वप्राणिनां सूक्ष्मस्थूलशरीरादेव सृष्टिः कृता। स्थूलशरीरं दृष्टं सूक्ष्मशरीरम् अदृष्टं च भवति। जीविवस्तुनोः

भौतिकशरीरं स्थूलं प्राणाः सूक्ष्माश्चं भवन्ति। वास्तुपुरुषः सूक्ष्मशरीरः भवति। तस्य वासस्थलं स्थूलमपि भवति। सामान्यजनानां बोधनार्थं प्रवृत्तो निगूढवेदान्तसंहितायाः ललितपरिश्रम एव वस्तुपुरुषसङ्कल्पः इत्यपि वक्तुं शक्यते।

वास्तुशास्त्रस्य पञ्चविभागाः सन्ति। तत्वशास्त्रं, सङ्ककल्पः नियमाः, प्रमाणानि, आचाराः च। तत्वशास्त्रम्-अहं ब्रह्मास्मि इति चिन्तया एव गृहनिर्माणं करणीयम्।

सङ्कल्पः-प्रपञ्चसङ्कल्पः वासतुपुरुषसङ्कल्पः च।

नियमाः-पादविन्यासः विधिनिर्णयः च ग्राह्यम्।

प्रमाणानि-स्थ्तलव्याप्तिः। सीमातःगृहपर्यन्तं स्थलम्, निर्माणस्थलव्याप्तिः च।

समराङ्गणसुत्रधारस्य पञ्चत्रिंशदध्याये शिलान्यासविधिः प्रतिपादितः।
शिलान्यासाय शिलायाः लक्षणम् गुणदोषविचिन्तनं च।

शिलामाद्यां विचक्षणः परीक्षेत। कुम्भ-अङ्कुश-ध्वज, छत्र-मत्स्य-चामर-तोरण-दुर्वा-नागफल-उष्णीष-पुष्प-स्वस्तिक-वेदिभिः, नन्द्यावर्त्तै स चामरैः कूर्मपद्मनिशाकरैः प्रशस्तैः प्राकरैः भूषिताः कर्मणः हिताः। दीर्घाः ह्रस्वाः अल्पविषमाः आच्छाभाः अध्माताः अपरीक्षिताः दिङ्मूढाः सास्थ्यङ्गाराः सशर्कराः अंगहीनाः दुःपक्वनिर्भिन्नाः कृष्णाः खण्डाः दोषभयावहाः नृणां पशुतुरंगाणां पदाङ्काः स्वस्तिः-वृद्धये। क्रव्यान् मृगविहङ्गानां पादैः स्पृष्टांस्तु वर्जयेत्।

शिलाः चतुर्विधाः -नन्दा, भद्रा, जया, पूर्णा-इति। ताः एव वासिष्ठी, काश्यपी, भार्गवी, आंगिरसी इति च कथ्यन्ते। तत्र प्रागुत्तरे देशे सन्निवेशस्य वास्तुनः नैर्ऋत्यां वा सकुसुमां समां गोचर्मसम्मितां सुगन्धकलशां चतुरश्रां वेदीं प्रकल्पयेत्। आग्नेय्यमादितः नन्दां शिलां क्रमशः स्थापयेत्। सपद्मोत्पलपलवैः सर्वौषधिहिरण्याद्यैः हेमरजतमृन्मयैः ताम्रमयैः कुम्भैः अकालभूलैः अव्यङ्गैः मन्त्रैः ताम् अभिषेचयेत्। तीर्थप्रस्रवणाम्भोभिः सरत्नाक्षतपङ्कजैः सुगन्धिभिः सपुण्याहम् अभिषेकं प्रयोजयेत्। जाह्नवी, यमुना, रेवा, सरस्वती इत्यादि संभवं महानदीजलं शस्तम्। शुभतीर्थभवं तथा

अद्रिवनवेशन्त देवायतनजानि च अभिषेकार्थम् अम्भांसि यथालाभमुपाहरेत्। अनेन मन्त्रेण च एतासाम् अभिषेकं समाचरेत्। हिरण्यवर्णाः पावन्यः शुचयः दुरितच्छिदः पुनन्तु शान्ताः श्रीमत्य आपः युष्मन् मधुच्युतः इति मन्त्रपूतेन पयसा ततः शिलाम् स्थापयित्वा स्थपतिः गन्धकल्केन माङ्गल्येन अनुलेपयेत्। हिचन्दनपूर्णेन सुगन्धिना व्यवकीर्य पुष्पदामभिः धूपमाल्योपहारैः सलाजैः च दधि-मांस-अक्षदादिभिः तरसा एनां छादयेत्। पुष्कलैः वस्त्रयुग्मैः च इष्टकां देवीं पूजयेत्। निवेशनान्ते नैर्ऋत्यां तदा अवस्थितान् समसंख्यान् शुचीन् प्राज्ञान् विप्रान् दक्षिणाफलैः अर्चयेत्। ओङ्कारस्वस्तिपुण्याहगीतवादित्रनिस्वनैः जनितरोमाञ्चः कर्ता तेभ्यः नमस्क्रियाम् कुर्यात्। वास्तोष्पयते भूतेभ्यः च ततः बलिं निवेद्य तासां चतसृणामन्याः उपशिलाः पृथक् कुर्यात्। प्राकारस्वस्तिकाङ्के द्वे तथा श्रीवत्सलक्षणा। नन्द्यावर्तस्तु पूर्णायां भवेत् एकः यथाक्रमम्। कोणे प्राग्दक्षिणे नन्दां वास्तुनः अधः स्थापयेत्। अन्याः क्रमेण भद्राद्याः कोणेष्वन्येषु च त्रिषु। प्रतिष्ठापनमन्त्राः च तासां चतसृणामपि। चत्वार ऋषिभिः गीता शाश्वतारम्भदर्शनाः। वीर्येण आदिवराहस्य वेदार्थैस्त्वभिमन्त्रिता वसिष्ठनन्दिनीं नन्दां प्राक् प्रतिष्ठापयाम्हम्। सुमुहूर्ते सुदिवसे सा त्वं नन्दे निवेशिता।

'आयुः कारयितुर्दीर्घं श्रियं चाग्रयामिहावह।
भद्रासि सर्वतोभद्रा भद्रे। भद्रं विधीयताम्।।
कश्यपस्य प्रियसुते! श्रीरस्तु गृहमेधिनः।
जये! विजयतां स्वामी गृहस्यास्य महात्मनः।।
आचन्द्रार्कं यशश्चास्य भूम्यामिह विरोहतु।
त्वयि सम्पूर्णचन्द्राभे! न्यस्तायां वास्तुनस्थले।।
भवत्येष गृहस्वामी पूर्णे! पूर्णमनोरथः।

इति स्वस्तिकवाचनैः मन्त्रैः मूलचयं कुर्यात्। ताभिः हिरण्यवर्णाभिः शिलाभिः सममद्भुतम्। प्रागुदक्प्लवना धन्या न प्रत्यग्दक्षिणाप्लवा। इष्टका चैत्यभवनप्रकारपुरकर्मसु विताने चितिविन्यासे चतुर्मुखनिकेतने पुरोधा शान्तिवेदीषु प्रतिमास्थापनेषु च। याज्ञिकेन विधानेन क्रमशः स्थापयेच्छिलाः। त्रैशोकौर्णासभासैस्ताः सामभिः स महाव्रतैः गायत्र्युष्णिगनुष्टुब्भिर्बृहत्या च।

यत्तु चयान् समस्थांश्चिनुतया चतुरः विरमेत्। ततः चितेः चतुष्टयं भित्तिप्रमाणं च ज्ञात्वा आदिकर्मैवं समाप्यम्। यथोत्तरं च कनिष्ठं प्रथमं भूतले प्रतिष्ठिताः सुस्थिताः समाः न चालयेत्। चालने गृहभर्तुः महत् भयं स्यात्। एतासां स्थिरतां स्थपतेः गृहभूर्तुः च परमं मङ्गलं विदुः। प्राग्दक्षिणायां चालने गृहभुर्तुः महद् भयम्। नैऋत्यां चालने गृहभर्तुः भार्याविनाशः मरुद्दिशि भीतिः। ऐशान्यां गुरोः च भयम्। प्रथमं स्थापितेनैवं स्तंभानपि न चालयेत्। नोद्धरेत प्रणुद्याच्च विधिः तुल्यः यतोऽनयोः। तस्मात् सम्यक् समाहितः शिलानां स्तंभानां च स्थपतिः सर्वथा द्वारप्राकारशालानां नगराणां वेश्मनां च निर्माणं कुर्यात्।

अधुनापि गृहादिनिर्माणे गृहभर्त्ता स्वस्वमतोक्तरीत्या देवतापूजां करोति। कर्मणो निर्विघ्नपरिसमाप्तिः देवताप्रसादेन भवति इति विश्वासः। कालभेदेन रीतिभेदोऽस्ति कर्मसु। परन्तु तत्वतो नास्ति भेदः।

Contributors

1.	Smt. P. Vasumathy Devi	:	Lecturer, Department of History, University of Kerala.
2.	Dr. K.G. Sreelekha	:	Professor & Head, ORI & Mss. Library, University of Kerala, Kariavattom.
3.	Dr. V. Rajeev	:	Asso. Professor, Catholicate College, Pathanamthiatta.
4.	Dr. Philip John	:	Asso. Professor, Devamatha College, Kuravilangad.
5.	Dri. Desikom Reghunadhan	:	Professor (Rtd.), M.G. College, Thiruvananthapuram.
6.	Sri. Manoj S. Nair	:	Consultant Engineer, Vasthuvidya, Gurukulam, Aranmula
7.	Maciej Karasinski	:	Research Scholar
8.	Sheeja K.P.	:	Assistant Professor, Government Engineering College, Kulathoor.
9.	Dr. G. Reghukumar	:	Assistant Professor SSUS, Thiruvananthapuram.
10.	Dr. Lalu S. Kurup	:	Assistant Professor, NSS College, Nilamel.
11.	Dr. K.S. Bindusree	:	Assistant Professor, University College, Thiruvananthapuram.

12.	Vysakh, A.S.	:	Research Scholar, Department of History, University of Kerala.
13.	Gopakumar, A.	:	Research Scholar, Department of ORI & Mss. Library.
14.	Jenusha, K.S.	:	Research Scholar, Department of Archaeology, Kariavattom.
15.	Renjith Rajan	:	Research Scholar, Department of Sanskrit.
16.	Ambily C.S.	:	Research Scholar, Department of Archaeology, Dariavattom.
17.	Kiran, A.U.	:	Research Scholar, Department of Sanskrit.
18.	Dr. Naduvattom Gopalakrishnan	:	Senior Fellow ISDL, Trivandrum.
19.	Dr. S.S. Sreekumar	:	Asso. Professor, MGGA College, New Mahe.
20.	Smt. J.M. Gandhimathi	:	Curator, Government Museum, Chennai.
21.	Krishnakumar, P.	:	Research Scholar, Department of ORI & Mss. Library.